<u>It's another Quality Book from CGP</u>

This book is for 7-11 year olds.

Whatever subject you're doing it's the same
old story — there are lots of facts and you've just got
to learn them. KS2 ICT is no different.

Happily this CGP book gives you all that important
information as clearly and concisely as possible.

It's also got some daft bits in to try and make the whole
experience at least vaguely entertaining for you.

<u>What CGP is all about</u>

Our sole aim here at CGP is to produce the highest quality books
— carefully written, immaculately presented and dangerously
close to being funny.

Then we work our socks off to get them out to you
— at the cheapest possible prices.

Contents

SECTION ONE — WORD PROCESSING

Changing The Text 1
Capital Letters and Layout 2
Moving Text... 3
Correcting Text 4
Find and Replace 5
Spellcheckers 6
Inserting Pictures 7
Keeping Your Work 8
What Can We Use Word Processing For? 9

SECTION TWO — GRAPHICS

Painting Software 10
Changing Pictures 11
Importing Pictures... 12
Drawing Software 13
Modelling 15

SECTION THREE — MULTIMEDIA PRESENTATIONS

Multimedia Software 16
Buttons 17
Linking Pages 18
Recording and Storing Sound 19
Music Software 20

SECTION FOUR — E-MAIL & THE INTERNET

E-mail 22
Sending E-mails 23
Attachments.. 24
Using the Internet for Research.. 25
Search Engines 26
More Searching and Finding.. 27
Hyperlink Buttons 28
Bookmarking Sites 29
Copying and Pasting Stuff... 30
Using The Information 31

SECTION FIVE — USING DATABASES

Organising Information 32
Records and Fields 33
Databases 34
Questionnaires 35
Adding and Sorting Information 36
Searching Databases 37
Drawing Graphs 38
Tree Diagrams 40

Shapes of Tree Diagrams 41
Branching Databases 42

SECTION SIX — ANALYSING DATA

Doing Database Searches 43
AND and OR Searches 44
Searching the Internet 45
Testing Ideas 46
Database Accuracy... 47
Checking for Accuracy 48
Checking for Accuracy Using Graphs.. 49

SECTION SEVEN — USING SPREADSHEETS

Budgets... 50
Spreadsheets 51
Formulas 52
Maths with Spreadsheets 54
Creating Graphs 55

SECTION EIGHT — SIMULATIONS

What are Simulations?... 56
Finding Patterns.. 57
The Floor Turtle... 58
Using LOGO 59
Repeating Things... 60
Procedures 61

SECTION NINE — MONITORING CONDITIONS

Monitoring 62
Using Sensors 63
Datalogging 64

SECTION TEN — CONTROLLING DEVICES

Instructions 66
Inputs and Outputs 67
Repeat and Wait 68
Controlling Lots of Outputs.. 70
Control Devices 72
Automatic Doors 73
Problems Caused By Errors 74

Index 75

Published by Coordination Group Publications

Contributors:
Charley Darbishire
Sharon Keeley
Simon Little
Becky May
Andy Park
Alan Rix
Glenn Rogers
Rachel Selway
Claire Thompson
Chrissy Williams

With thanks to Diane Murray and Katherine Reed for the proof-reading.

ISBN   1 84146 455 4

Groovy website: www.cgpbooks.co.uk
Jolly bits of clipart from CorelDRAW
Printed by Elanders Hindson, Newcastle upon Tyne.

With thanks to Microsoft, Logotron, Expressive Software Projects; Granada
Learning; and Data Harvest for permission to use screenshots from MS Word,
MS Excel, MS Paint, MS Explorer, MSW LOGO and Outlook Express; Junior
Viewpoint; Compose World Junior; Granada Branch; and Graph and Meter
respectively.

Changing The Text

There are *Loads of Ways* to Change How *Words Look*

I've changed the <u>size</u> of letters.

People water **plants** to make them gr⁰**W**.

Some people water **evil witches** to make them **S̷h̷r̷i̷v̷e̷l** up.

Clouds water *sunshine* to make rainbow$.

I've changed <u>colours</u>.

I've changed the <u>font</u> of words.

You make words <u>stand out</u> by making them **bold**, *italic* or <u>underlined</u>. ***Or all three***.

This text is bold.   *This text is italic*.   <u>This text is underlined</u>.   ***This text is all three***.

Use The *Text Toolbar* to Change How *Words Look*

The <u>first</u> thing you have to do is <u>highlight</u> the bit of text you want to change.

Hold the <u>left</u> mouse button down and <u>drag</u> the cursor.

The purple pansy-eater squelched through the mud.

Now use the <u>text toolbar</u> to change this text.

<u>Click</u> on the little <u>down arrows</u> (▼) to see the <u>other</u> fonts, sizes and colours.

These three buttons make your text **bold**, *italic* or <u>underlined</u>.

Normal	▼ Times New Roman	▼ 10	▼	**B** *I* <u>U</u>	≡ ≡ ≡ ≡	⋮≡ ⋮≡ ⋱ ⋱	▦ ▼ · ✎ ▼ · **A** ▼

You can change the <u>font</u> here.

This changes the <u>size</u> of the letters.

You can choose the <u>colour</u> of the text here.

Be bold and make your words look cool...

One of the great things about word processing is that you can experiment with heaps of different fonts in different sizes and colours. If you don't like it — you can just change it back. Remember to highlight the words you want to change before you make the changes.

Capital Letters and Layout

Hold down Shift to get Capital Letters

If you want a capital letter, hold down the shift key and press the letter you want.
For example, to get a capital A:

⇧ + A = A

The shift key normally looks like this.

You also need to hold down the shift key to get some punctuation marks and special symbols.

⇧ + ?/ = ?   ⇧ + £3 = £

You can Change the Alignment of the Text

Alignment is where the words line up on the page.
There might be buttons like this on the toolbar.

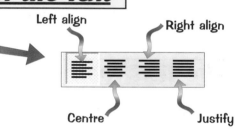

Left align   Right align

Centre   Justify

This text is on the left

This text is **left align**ed. This text is **left align**ed. ←
This text is **left align**ed. This text is ←
left aligned. ←

This text is on the right

→ This text is **right align**ed. This text is **right align**ed.
→ This text is **right align**ed. This text is
→ **right align**ed.

This text is in the middle

→ This text is **centre align**ed. This text is **centre align**ed. ←
→ This text is **centre align**ed. This text is ←
→ **centre align**ed. ←

This text is justified

This text is **justified**. This text is **justified**. This text is **justified**.
This text is **justified**. This text is **justified**. This text is **justified**.
This text is **justified**. This text is **justified**. This text is **justified**.

Be neat and tidy — align your text...

If you're going to get anywhere with word processing, you need to know how to type
capital letters — they're vital for starting sentences and names. Also, try out the different
ways of aligning text and you'll see it makes a big difference to how the finished text looks.

Moving Text

'Copy' Picks up a Copy of the Text — 'Paste' puts it down

There's a really easy way to repeat something you've typed.

1) Highlight the words you want to repeat.

2) Click on 'Copy'.

3) Click where you want the copied text to go.

4) Click 'Paste' to place the copy.

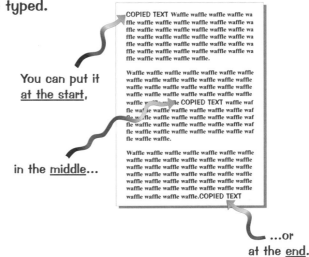

You can put it at the start,

in the middle...

...or at the end.

You can also copy and paste text from one file to another and from one program to another.

Use 'Cut' and 'Paste' to Move Things Around

Cut and paste makes it easy to put things in the right order.

 1 Highlight the words you want to move. Then click on 'Cut'.

 The words disappear.

Just pull yourself together.
Doctor, doctor!
I feel like a pair of curtains.

 2 Click the cursor where you want to put the words.

Doctor, doctor!
I feel like a pair of curtains.

3 Click on 'Paste'.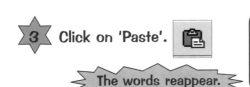

The words reappear.

Doctor, doctor!
I feel like a pair of curtains.
Just pull yourself together.

Copy and paste — the smarter way to write lines...

The copy, cut and paste tools are really easy to use and they make moving and copying text dead quick. Most computers have shortcut buttons for them on the toolbar (that look like the buttons shown on this page), but if not, you can find copy, cut and paste in the Edit menu.

Correcting Text

There are easy ways to add, change and delete words.

Adding Words

Add words by clicking the cursor somewhere and typing.

Changing Words

Change a whole word by double-clicking on it to highlight it.
When you type the new word, the original word will disappear.

Deleting Words

Deleting words means removing them. You can either:

⭐ Delete a whole word by highlighting it and then pressing 'Backspace',

or ⭐ Delete one letter at a time by clicking the cursor
somewhere and pressing 'Backspace'.

This is the 'Backspace' key — it might have an arrow on it:

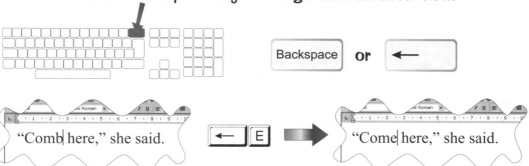

Backspace **or** ←

"Comb here," she said. ← E ➡ "Come here," she said.

Changing words can be very ~~exciting~~ useful...

Everyone makes mistakes when they're typing — so it's useful to know how to go back and
correct text quickly and easily. Also, you can make your writing much more interesting by
going back and adding some good descriptive words. Adding words couldn't be easier...

Find and Replace

You can use 'Find' and 'Replace' to make lots of changes to a document.

'Find and Replace' is Great for Fixing Lots of Mistakes

This is part of a very <u>long</u> story about Ally.

But Ally isn't a boy, she's a <u>girl</u>.
And Ally isn't a dog, she's a <u>cat</u>.

 Woof

Ally is the name of my dog. He's a very good dog. He's black, and he likes sitting on my lap. When I'm in the kitchen, he asks me to give him food.

I need to make some <u>changes</u>.

he ⟶ she
him ⟶ her
dog ⟶ cat

If I made all the changes myself, it would take a <u>long time</u>, and I'd probably <u>miss some</u>.

Use 'Replace' to Swap One Word for Another

A computer can change 'he' to 'she' everywhere in the story very <u>quickly</u>.

1 Go to the '<u>Edit</u>' menu, and click on '<u>Replace</u>'.

2 I want to change '<u>he</u>' to '<u>she</u>'.

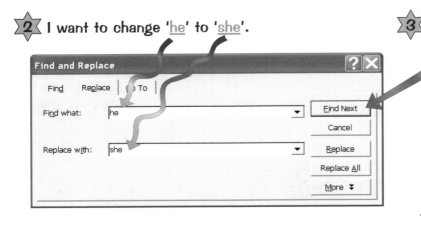

3 It's usually best to use '<u>Find Next</u>' (and <u>not</u> 'Replace All').
Then you can check that the computer's <u>not getting confused</u> and changing the wrong thing.

- I <u>don't</u> want to change this one — so I click on '<u>Find Next</u>'.

'he' is part of the word 'the'

Ally is the name of my dog. A
He's black, and he likes sitti

- But I <u>do</u> want to change this one — so I click on '<u>Replace</u>'.

y dog. He's a very good dog.
es sitting on my lap. When

Use 'Find' and 'Replace' to save yourself loads of work...

'Find and replace' is quick and doesn't miss any words. BUT, it can change words you don't want to change, so you have to check it. It's sometimes OK to use 'Replace All', if you're sure that the word you want to replace won't be part of another word.

Section One — Word Processing

Spellcheckers

Computers can help you spell things <u>correctly</u>.

Spellcheckers Help You Find Mistakes...

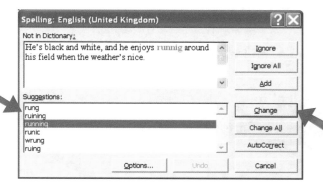

Sometimes the mistakes are <u>underlined</u> automatically.

Sometimes you have to click on the <u>spellcheck button</u>. It might look like this one:

...But You Still Need to Know How to Spell

Spellcheckers usually ask you to <u>choose</u> the correct spelling from a list.

Click on the <u>correct spelling</u> and then click on '<u>Change</u>'.

Spellcheckers Can't Always Help

Spellcheckers are good... but they <u>can't</u> find every mistake.

The name of my friend's coat is Bob.

A spellchecker won't know that you mean '<u>goat</u>' — not '<u>coat</u>'.
'Coat' is a <u>real word</u>, so the spellchecker thinks it's okay.
You need to make sure yourself that the text <u>makes sense</u>.

Thare's sumfing rong wif mi spelchekur...

Spellcheckers are really useful, but only if you don't become too reliant on them. You need to be able to find spelling mistakes yourself too, because the spellchecker won't pick all of them up. Read each sentence to check it makes sense, even after you've done a spellcheck.

Inserting Pictures

It's easy to _insert pictures_ into your documents, and it instantly _jazzes things up_ a bit.

Pictures can be _Photos_, _Artwork_ or _Cartoons_

A photograph

A drawing

A cartoon from Clipart

Putting in a _Clipart_ Picture

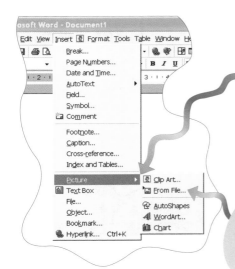

Open the 'Insert' menu.
Go to 'Picture', then to 'Clipart'.

You'll get a _menu_ with loads of pictures to choose from.

Click on the picture you want and press the _open_ or _insert_ button.

Open

To put in your own picture or photo, choose 'From File...' instead of 'Clip Art'.

You'll need to know the filename of your picture.

You can _Change_ the _Size_ of your _Picture_

Select the picture by _clicking_ on it to make _little squares_ (called 'handles') appear.

Drag the corner ones out or in to make the picture bigger or smaller.

Drag the side ones out or in to squash or stretch the picture.

A picture tells a thousand words — so insert one...

Inserting pictures makes your documents look cool — people would rather look at something with colourful pictures than a page of solid black-and-white text. Once a picture's in the document it needs to look right, so play around with the handles until it's the right size.

Keeping Your Work

Remember to Save Your Work

Saving your work will store it safely in the computer.

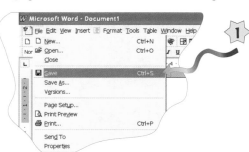

1 Open the 'File' menu. Go to 'Save'.

You might need to find the right folder to save your work in.

2 The computer will ask you what you want your work to be called. Give it a sensible name so you can find it again.

3 Click 'Save'.

Sometimes it's nice to keep lots of different drafts of your work.
Use 'Save As' to save a new version without deleting the old version.
Remember to give your new draft a different name.

◄ Boring Poem_zz border

'Save As' is in the 'File' menu, underneath 'Save'.

◄ Boring Poem_diamond border

To open up your work later, click on the 'Open' button and look for your file.

You Can Print Your Work too

It's really easy to print out your work.
Just click on the 'Print' button,
which looks something like this

Another way of printing is to go to the 'File' menu and choose print.

Save yourself from disaster — save your work...

It's really important to save your work. If you don't, the moment the program's closed, your work will be gone — for ever. You need to save it often, not just when you've finished. Then if the computer suddenly crashes, you won't have lost all your work.

What Can We Use Word Processing For?

You can do <u>loads</u> of things with word processing — it's dead handy. Here are a few ideas.

<u>Use</u> Text and Pictures <u>To Show How To</u> Make Things

You can produce <u>instructions</u> for how to make something.

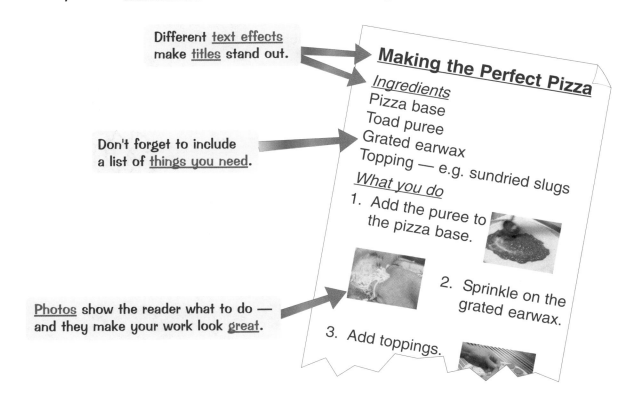

Different <u>text effects</u> make <u>titles</u> stand out.

Don't forget to include a list of <u>things you need</u>.

<u>Photos</u> show the reader what to do — and they make your work look <u>great</u>.

Making the Perfect Pizza

<u>Ingredients</u>
Pizza base
Toad puree
Grated earwax
Topping — e.g. sundried slugs

<u>What you do</u>
1. Add the puree to the pizza base.
2. Sprinkle on the grated earwax.
3. Add toppings.

<u>Designing</u> Packaging <u>is Easy too</u>

The <u>name</u> of the product is in <u>large</u>, <u>colourful text</u>.

<u>Pictures</u> show what's inside the package.

Information about the product is in <u>smaller text</u>.

A <u>logo</u> shows who made the product.

Sun-Dried Slug Pizza

Only £1.99

Not suitable for vegetarians. May contain soil.

Nutritious and delicious. Contains vitamins and minerals.

Grotty Grub Ltd.

<u>It's not all words, words, words, you know...</u>

Word processing is not the best name, because you can do loads more stuff with it than just write words. People use word processing software to create all kinds of things that include a mixture of words and pictures, such as packaging, posters, adverts, instructions, maps...

Painting Software

You can use <u>painting software</u> to mess about with pictures and make cool <u>patterns</u>.

'Copy' and 'Paste' Help you Make Repeating Patterns

<u>Copy</u> and <u>Paste</u> are in the <u>Edit</u> menu at the top.

Clicking on Copy and then on Paste will make <u>another</u> copy of whatever was selected...

...and clicking on Paste again and again will make <u>lots more copies</u>.

E.g. you could make some attractive chicken wallpaper.

If you have a <u>stamper</u> tool, you can just <u>click</u> where you want your pictures to be.

Use the Brush Tool to Make a Picture out of Dots

1) You can paint dots with the <u>Brush Tool</u>.

2) Change the <u>thickness</u> or <u>shape</u> of the brush for different effects.

Small dots give the chicken speckles.

Round dots make a fluffy chicken.

Lines make spiky grass

You need never get covered in paint again — shame...

There are so many things you can make if you know how to do repeating patterns — wallpaper, wrapping paper, pretty borders for schoolwork, pictures of thousands and thousands of assorted creepy crawlies to scare little brothers, mums and teachers (if you dare)...

Changing Pictures

Remember — you can mess about with parts of a picture, but you'll have to <u>select</u> them first.

The <u>Select Tool</u> looks like 🔲

1) Choose the <u>Select tool</u>.
2) <u>Click</u> and <u>hold</u> the mouse button down to <u>drag a box</u> round part of the picture.

Click and hold here.

The bit inside the box is selected.

Drag to here and let go of the button.

3) Now you can Copy and Paste to make a <u>copy</u> of whatever you selected.

Use <u>Flip/Rotate</u> to make Different <u>Reflections</u>

In Microsoft Paint, the '<u>Flip/Rotate</u>' tool turns things <u>upside down</u> and <u>spins</u> things round.

It's in the '<u>Image</u>' menu.

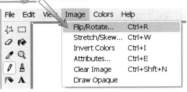

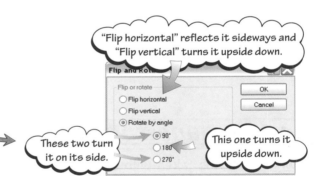

"Flip horizontal" reflects it sideways and "Flip vertical" turns it upside down.

1) Click on 'Flip/Rotate' and you'll get a window like this:
2) Click on the thing you want.
3) Hit the OK button.

These two turn it on its side.

This one turns it upside down.

Oops! Hit the wrong button? Press <u>Undo</u>...

If you make a mistake:
1) Find the <u>Undo</u> button (↺) at the top of the screen.
2) If there isn't one, find it in the '<u>Edit</u>' menu.
3) Click on it to <u>cancel whatever you did last</u> — magic.

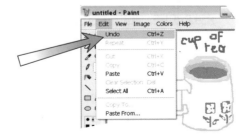

These tools are flipping marvellous...

Flip/Rotate means you can create fancy graphics quickly — e.g. you can make <u>symmetrical</u> <u>patterns</u> by reflecting shapes. And Undo works in almost any program — it's the best trick ever.

Importing Pictures

You <u>don't</u> always have to draw pictures <u>from scratch</u>.
You can <u>import</u> (add) pictures from <u>other places</u> into your document.

You can Import Pictures from Clip-Art

Importing means adding something that was made in <u>another software program</u>.

① To import clip-art into <u>MS Paint</u>, go to the '<u>Edit</u>' menu and click on '<u>Paste From</u>'.

② Then you'll get a window like this:

Find the <u>clip-art file</u> that you want to import and click on it. Then click on '<u>Open</u>'.

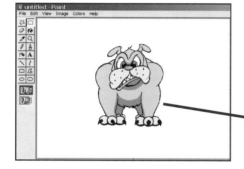

③ Then <u>click on the page</u> where you want the picture to go, and it will appear. Now you can <u>resize</u> it and <u>move</u> it about the page, as you wish.

You Can Also Import Photos from Digital Cameras

You can <u>download</u> photos taken with a <u>digital camera</u> onto the computer and save them as <u>picture files</u>.

Then just follow the <u>same steps</u> as for importing clip-art, and you get a lovely photo of your <u>gorgeous, slobbering dog</u> (or whatever).

You can also use a scanner to scan photos, hand-drawings or pictures from books, magazines etc. Then you can import the saved files in the same way.

Importing is great — especially if you can't draw...

Importing pictures means that you can create more complicated pictures — because you've already got a base that you can then make changes to. Don't forget that you can import all kinds of picture files — digital photos, scanned pictures or photos, clip-art...

Drawing Software

Painting software is good for some things. But for others, a <u>drawing program</u> is better.

You Can Use 'Word' as a Drawing Program

<u>Microsoft Word</u> is a word processor. But you can use it as a drawing program too.

1 Have the '<u>Drawing Toolbar</u>' on screen when you're making pictures.

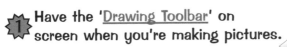

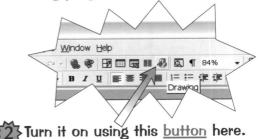

2 Turn it on using this <u>button</u> here.

Drawing Programs are Object-Based

Drawing programs are often called <u>object-based programs</u> — anything you draw is an <u>object</u>.

Just click here for a line...   ...here for a square or rectangle...

...or here for a circle or an oval.

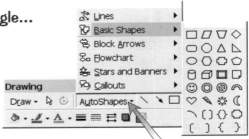

Or click on '<u>Autoshapes</u>' for more fancy shapes.

Just Click and Drag

Drawing programs are usually pretty <u>easy to use</u>.

1 <u>Select</u> the shape you want on the toolbar...

2 ...<u>click</u> on the page and hold down the mouse button...

3 ...then <u>drag out</u> a shape.

Drawing shapes doesn't need to be a drag...

Word is really good when you just need to draw simple shapes. The program does all the work for you — you just choose your shape, then click and drag to show where on the page you want it to go and how big you want it to be. Simple.

Drawing Software

Once you've made a shape, you can easily <u>change how it looks</u> with a drawing program.

Select the Object you want to Change

Before you can change anything about an object, you'll have to <u>select</u> it by clicking on it.

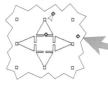

1 Selecting a shape makes white handles appear which you can drag to <u>change its size and shape</u> in cool ways.

2 You can easily rearrange shapes on the page. To <u>move a shape</u> — just select it and drag it.

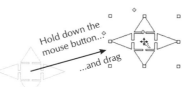
Hold down the mouse button... ...and drag

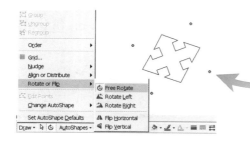

3 You can <u>rotate shapes</u> by clicking on 'Draw', then 'Rotate or Flip'. If you click on 'Free Rotate', you get little green handles to drag.

Object-Based Programs Use 'Layers'

With an object-based <u>drawing package</u>, you can put objects behind or in front of other objects.

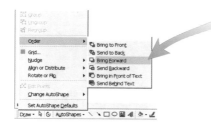

In Word, you can move an object from one layer to another by clicking on '<u>Draw</u>' then '<u>Order</u>'.

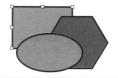
1 You draw 3 shapes on top of each other and select the rectangle...

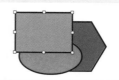
2 ...then you can move it to the front.

Order, order — 1 object, your honour...

Once you've selected an object, you can do loads of other things to it, as well as changing its shape. For example, if you're using Microsoft Word, you can add arrow heads to lines, make shapes 3D, add shadows, plus loads more cool things — play around and see what you can do.

Modelling

Model **Your** Classroom with Drawing Software

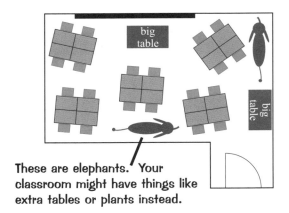

These are elephants. Your classroom might have things like extra tables or plants instead.

1) This is a model of a <u>classroom</u> for 20 students.

2) It's <u>drawn to a scale</u> of 1 centimetre to 1 metre (1 cm on the model shows 1 metre of the real classroom).

> I can move all the shapes around on screen, so I can see what different desk arrangements will look like, without actually moving any furniture.

Models Can Help You Solve Problems

<u>Two extra students</u> are joining the class, so I need more desks and chairs. I can try out different furniture arrangements using the model.

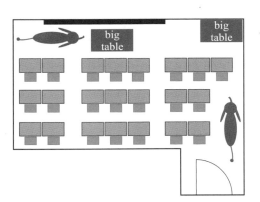

Desks that 4 students can sit around are better. Also, I'll get rid of one of the big tables and both the elephants.

This model is very <u>crowded</u>.

OR

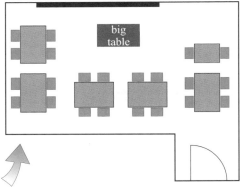

1) This is <u>much better</u>.
2) It means buying new tables.
3) But at least I know it'll be <u>worth it</u>.

If you can't be a supermodel, be a super-modeller...

Modelling comes in really handy for all kinds of things, especially saving money. It means you can see how things will look in real life, without <u>actually</u> having to try them out and pay for them. Then you can choose the best option from your models and do that one in real life.

Multimedia Software

Multimedia software can do loads of things. It can play sounds and music, show videos, pictures and animations, and do a zillion other cool things.

Multimedia Software can do Loads of Stuff

CD-ROMs and Internet web pages use multimedia. Multimedia pages are often interactive — you make things happen by clicking on the buttons.

Advantages of Multimedia:

1. Fun.
2. Easy to use.
3. Interactive.
4. Quicker than using a book.

Disadvantages of Multimedia:

1. Difficult to carry computers around with you.
2. Computers are expensive.
3. Computers crash — books don't.

Multimedia Pages Should be Easy to Use

Multimedia web pages need to be easy to use.
These two pages use the same information, but they've been designed really differently.

 Bad Page

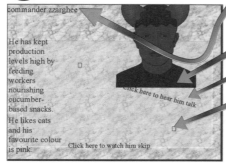

Title just looks like normal text.

Picture is too dark and the top is chopped off.

Text is messy.

It's hard to see where the buttons link to.

Good Page

Title is bigger so it stands out.

Picture is clearer and fits in nicely with the text.

Text is set out neatly.

Buttons are clearly labelled and easy to understand.

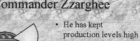

A tidy web page is a happy web page...

The basic rule is to keep your multimedia page looking neat and tidy at all times — planning how to use space is just as important as making it look pretty. If you try and cram too much in, then your page will look really squashed — it won't be clear and it will be hard to understand.

Buttons

Buttons, Hotspots and Hyperlinks are the same thing — you click on them and something happens.

Something Happens when you Click a Button

When you click on a button, one of these two things will happen:

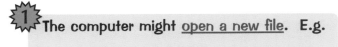

The computer might open a new file. E.g.

Open a sound file (i.e. play a sound).

Open a picture file (i.e. show a picture).

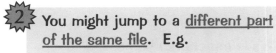

You might jump to a different part of the same file. E.g.

Jump to the next page of the document.

Jump to the homepage.

> A homepage is the 'first page' of a website — it says what the site is about, and usually has lots of links to other pages.

Draw a Button — then Link it to Something

To make a button you have to do these two things:

 Type a word, or draw a picture or shape — this will be your button.

 Select your button, and link it to a new file (or a different part of the same file) — you might need to click on the hyperlink button for this.

You'll see a menu something like this:

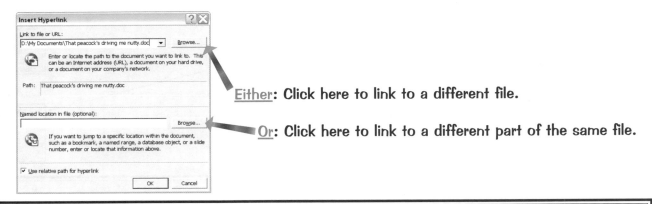

Either: Click here to link to a different file.

Or: Click here to link to a different part of the same file.

What happens if I press this red button? — oops...

Bet you thought linking different files would be really complicated — well it's not, in fact it's a piece of cake. Just draw your button, then link it to something else using the menu that comes up — and that's it, minimum faff involved.

Linking Pages

Buttons can also link different 'pages' together. 'Pages' could be completely <u>different documents</u>, or <u>different parts of the same document</u> — it depends on what software you're using.

Draw a 'Map' to Plan your Links

Before you start linking pages <u>willy-nilly</u>, it's good to draw a '<u>map</u>' to show all the links you need.

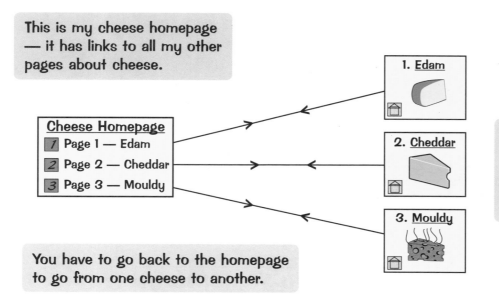

This is my cheese homepage — it has links to all my other pages about cheese.

Each page has a link back to the homepage.

The homepage button looks like a home — 🏠

You have to go back to the homepage to go from one cheese to another.

Make it Clear what the Buttons Do

I've made my cheese site and I've also added some <u>more links</u> — now you can read pages 1 to 3 <u>without</u> going to the homepage.

<u>The buttons are easy to understand</u>
This is because they:
 a) look the same on each page,
 b) are in the same place on every
     page (and are easy to find),
 c) are clearly labelled with symbols.

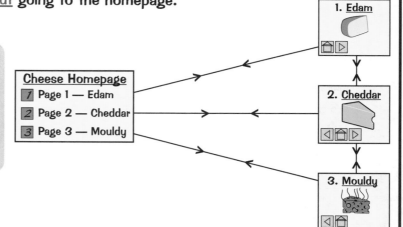

Oh dear, it's another cheesy pun...

Making a site like this is easy...
1) First you draw a 'map' of your website, showing how pages are linked.
2) Then you make all your pages.
3) And when you've done all that, you can link the pages together like on your map.

Recording and Storing Sound

You can record sounds for your multimedia pages using the Windows <u>Sound Recorder</u>.

Windows has its own Sound Recorder

This is how to find the Sound Recorder (your menus might look a little bit different).

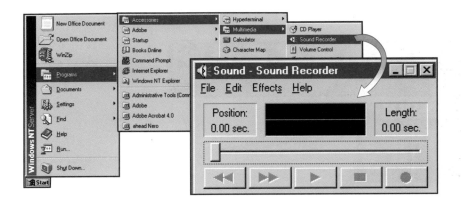

<u>Volume Control</u> is usually on the same menu.

Recording Sounds is Easy

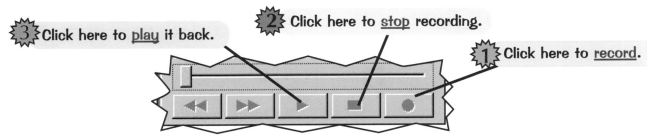

3 Click here to <u>play</u> it back.

2 Click here to <u>stop</u> recording.

1 Click here to <u>record</u>.

You'll need a <u>microphone</u> too. Your computer might have one <u>built in</u>, or you might need to <u>plug one in</u>.

Saving your Sounds is just as Simple

You can save your recording as a <u>sound file</u>.

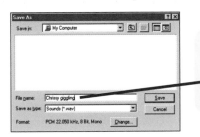

1. Click on 'Save As' in the File Menu.
2. Give your file a name.
3. Click on 'Save'.

Sound files are often stored on <u>CD-ROMs</u>.

To <u>play your sound file</u> go into Windows Explorer and double-click on the icon.

Mike's been a bit quiet lately...

Recording sound can be really useful, for example if you want to show something in a presentation. If you're having trouble recording something, check the microphone volume isn't set to 'Mute'. Do this on the volume control menu.

Music Software

You can Write Songs with Musical Pictures

Music software can make it really easy to compose tunes.
This one's called Compose World Junior.

Use these buttons to play your sequence in different ways.

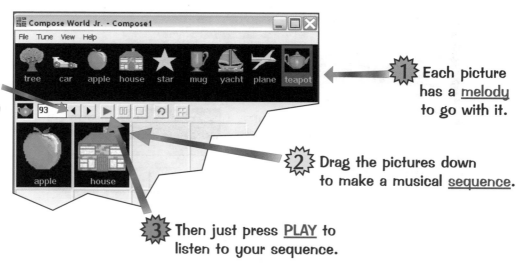

1 Each picture has a melody to go with it.

2 Drag the pictures down to make a musical sequence.

3 Then just press PLAY to listen to your sequence.

Changing Your Tune

1 You can change the tempo (how fast the music is played).

The tempo here is 93.

2 You can open new pictures and music.

On Compose World Junior, go to the File Menu and choose 'Open'.

These are all different picture sets. Each one has different music.

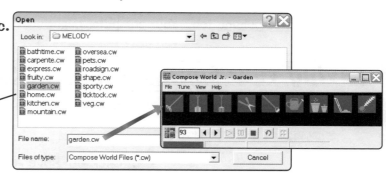

3 Choosing different instruments can make the same tune sound very different.

Go to the Tunes Menu and select Instruments.

Tone-deaf composers — whatever next...

Music programs are great — the pictures mean that you can build a song in chunks, like using musical building blocks. But best of all, you don't have to be musical to use them — you don't need to play the tune yourself, you just press the play button.

Music Software

Using the <u>same</u> pictures all the time can get boring.
Here are some different pictures, that can create <u>interesting music</u>:

 ## Pictures and Music with the Same Theme

Sometimes the <u>theme</u> of the pictures tells you what kind of music it is.

The tunes that go with these pictures all sound <u>oriental</u>.

 ## Pictures that Represent Different Moods

The music for each of these <u>weather</u> pictures matches the mood of the picture.

The music for <u>storm</u> is loud and menacing....

...but the music for <u>sunset</u> is quiet and relaxing.

 ## Proper Musical Notation

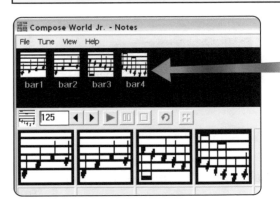

These pictures use proper musical notation. They show the <u>actual notes</u> being played.

This is how music is written for most <u>musical instruments</u>.

Make your music suit your mood

It's good to experiment with different pictures to try and give your tune a certain mood, e.g. a happy mood or a relaxing mood. When you've composed your tune, you can combine it with live music. Why not tape yourself singing along or playing an instrument alongside?

E-mail

E-mail lets you send messages to people with a computer which is connected to the Internet.

What's so Good about E-mail?

E-mail's great because:
1. It's really quick.
2. It's cheap.
3. You can use it in different places.

But E-mail's a pain because:
1. It's not secret — other people might read it.
2. It's not permanent (doesn't last for ever). Once you delete it — it's gone for good.
3. You have to type.

If you want people to send you e-mails, you need an e-mail address.
E-mail addresses look like this:

> name@blah.blah.uk

New E-mails go in the Inbox

Getting new e-mails is really exciting. The Inbox is where to look for new messages.

1 > Click on Inbox to open it.

2 > Click on an e-mail to read it.

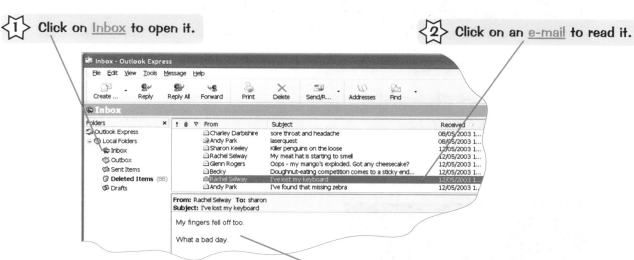

3 > Read the e-mails here.

You can print e-mails you want to keep. There'll probably be a button like this.

E-by-gum mail...

Most people and businesses use e-mail now because it's so much quicker than sending a letter. But it does have its disadvantages, and there's still something cool about receiving a letter in the post, so e-mail will probably never completely take over.

Sending E-mails

There are Four Stages to Sending an E-mail

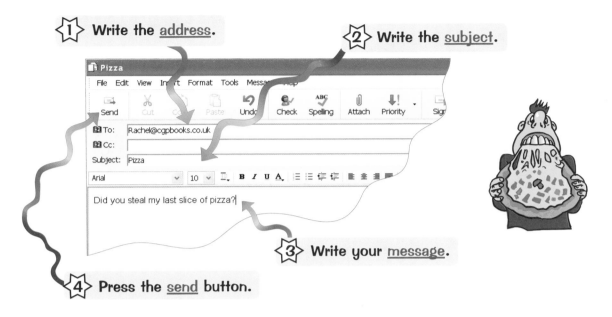

① Write the address.

② Write the subject.

③ Write your message.

④ Press the send button.

Replying is even easier. You don't have to type the person's address in.

Just click on reply.

Now you can get on with typing your message.

Keep E-mail Addresses in an Address Book

You can keep all your e-mail addresses in the address book. This means you can send messages without typing the address. Just click on the person's name.

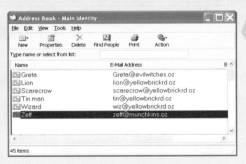

Sending e-mails is dead easy — bad news for postmen...

Sending and receiving e-mails is very straightforward once you know how.
The e-mail program shown in this book is 'Outlook Express', but all e-mail programs
do the same jobs, even if they look a bit different.

Attachments

You Can Attach Stuff to E-mails

It's great. You can send a picture to your friends or send a song to your Gran.
It's just ACE.

Here's what you do:

1) Write a message.

2) Click on the paperclip.

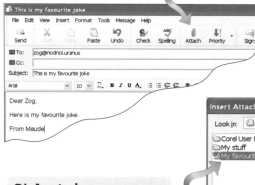

You need to find the right folder first.

3) A window appears.
   Click on the file you
   want to attach.

4) Click 'Attach'.   Easy.

You Can Attach Sounds, Pictures or Text Files to E-mails

This is what the
attachment looks like:

I'm very attached to this page...

Attachments are brill — you can send all kinds of things, like birthday cards, invitations,
instructions, a recorded message... and they get there almost straightaway — magic.
Be warned though, if you're sending a big file, it can take a bit longer to get through.

* Be warned — attaching live ducks with sellotape doesn't work. They'll peck you.

Using The Internet for Research

Doing research <u>used to mean</u> sitting in a library with loads of books and getting <u>bored</u>. Now there's the <u>Internet</u> — it's a cool way to find stuff out.

The Internet has Loads of Information

The Internet's great because:

There's a huge amount of information — much more than your local library.

The Internet's bad because:

There's <u>so</u> much information that it's hard to find useful stuff. Also, some of the information might be <u>biased.</u>

<u>Organisations</u>, such as museums and tourist offices, have websites where you can find <u>information</u> about them. Most <u>newspapers</u> have websites too.

Don't Trust Everything You Read on Websites

You can't always be sure information is <u>reliable</u> — especially on <u>websites</u>. <u>Anyone</u> can set up their own website and say <u>whatever they like</u>.

Information might be <u>biased</u>. Everyone has their own <u>opinion</u>, and might try to convince you that theirs is <u>right</u>.

Read these descriptions of the same event:

HOW I SURVIVED A CAT ATTACK

I was attacked by a cat for no reason. It bent my cage and stole my water bottle. I was really frightened by it all. I'm the victim here.

I WAS HIT BY AN EVIL HAMSTER

The evil hamster made me attack it. It threw its water bottle at my head and it hurt me so much I almost fainted. I don't remember much. I'm the victim here.

They can't both be true — you don't know what happened for sure.

Beware of biased information:
- ☆ Think about who wrote it and if there might be another side to the story.
- ☆ If in doubt, compare it with a different source.

No bias here... (psst, CGP books are the best in the world)

The Internet is seriously cool — no doubt about that. But you have to be careful, or it could have you believing all kinds of nonsense. Be suspicious of information and look out for bias.

Search Engines

Use a Search Engine to Find a Website

There are lots of different search engines you can use (e.g. Google, Yahoo, MSN, etc...), but they all look something like this:

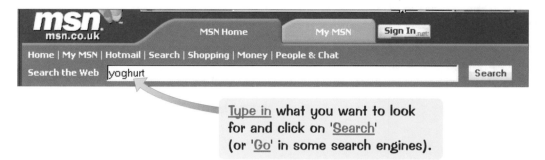

Type in what you want to look for and click on 'Search' (or 'Go' in some search engines).

Each Result is Called a Hit

In a few seconds the search engine will show you all the sites it found.

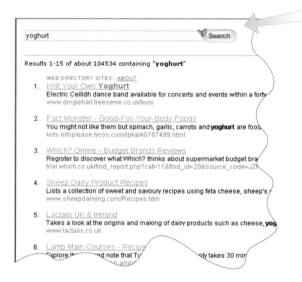

The main problem with these results is that there are so many of them.
In this example, there were 104 534 hits.

It would take ages to go through them all (and most of them would be useless anyway).

This isn't exactly what I had in mind...

Searches using one word are about as useful as putting a duck in an elephant suit.
You need to make your searches more precise (see page 27).

Search engines take you to websites — choo-choo...

The Internet is so huge that you need to use a search engine to find anything — it would take forever to find something just by trying out different possible website addresses.
The golden rule is not to search for one word only — instead, be more precise and detailed.

More Searching and Finding

Searching with just one word can be pretty useless —
the computer can only work with the information you give it.

Use the Word 'AND' in Your Searches

If you use the word 'AND' in your searches, it'll narrow down the results.

E.g. If you wanted to know about smelly cheeses, you could type this into the search box:

> smelly AND cheese

The search engine will only look for pages with both words in.

You can type in as many words as you like,
as long as you put 'AND' in between them.

This smells worse than your minging feet...

E.g. | smelly AND cheese AND french AND old | would narrow the results down even more.

Choose Your Words Carefully

Some words get better results than others. That's because they're more specific.
If you want to find out about a particular type of thing, then type its name in.

I like Gorgonzola

If I want to know about the size of a velociraptor's teeth, I'll get better
results by searching for "velociraptor AND teeth" than by typing "dinosaur".

Practise Skimming Through Results

Skimming means looking through lists of titles
quickly and judging if they look useful or not.

You searched for dinosaur **and** teeth
Sites 31 - 40 of 861, 571, 354, 416

31. Dinosaurs today — where can they be found in the wild now?
An online debate about where to go for the best dinosaur
spotting holiday.
www.wemakethisup.com

32. Romford Archaeological Museum
We have lots of ancient things for you to see.
www.romfordmuseum.com

No. 33 is a puzzle, so it won't have any information.

33. Dinosaur crossword puzzle.
Have bundles of fun with this puzzle..
http://www.dinosaur.co.uk/puzzle

No. 34 is about dentistry. I can ignore it.

34. History of Dentistry
Have you ever wanted to know where dentistry started?
We'll tell you anyway.
http://www.dentist.org.uk/history/please visit/please.com

35. How many teeth did the dinosaurs have?
We know and we'll tell you.
www.facts.co.uk

BOY: What's a velociraptor? INTERNET: Search me...

Using 'AND' between words makes your search more effective. The more 'ands' you use, the
better and your and results and will and be (tee hee, did I confuse you?). Also, practise
skimming — it's a great trick to learn because you can skip the useless hits and save time.

Hyperlink Buttons

You can also search the Internet by <u>clicking on buttons</u>...

You Can Use Hyperlink Buttons to Surf the Internet

Most websites have <u>buttons</u> on them that <u>link</u> to other web pages when you click on them.

- These are called <u>hyperlink buttons</u> (like on multimedia encyclopaedia CD-ROMs) and you can use them to jump from website to website.

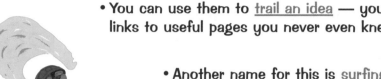

Music brings me out of my shell

- You can use them to <u>trail an idea</u> — you follow interesting links to useful pages you never even knew were there.

- Another name for this is <u>surfing the Internet</u>, which is weird because it's not wet and you don't use a board. But anyway...

My tortoise has started <u>singing</u> Westlife songs. I want to find a website that can tell me what's wrong with her. All I have is the <u>website address</u> for the place I bought her bedding from.

By following these <u>links</u>, I can <u>trail an idea</u> until I find a <u>link</u> to a page that is <u>useful</u>.

Let's See You Back Out of This One...

Clicking the '<u>Back</u>' button will take you back to the <u>previous page</u>.

Hyperlinks — buttons that have had too many sweets...

Using hyperlinks to surf the Internet is fine, as long as you keep focused on what it is that you actually want to find out — it's very easy to find yourself side-tracked. The computer records your route through websites, so you can always back-track by clicking the 'Back' button.

Bookmarking Sites

A URL is the Address of a Website

URLs are addresses of websites. They look a bit like this:

http://www.crazyinthecoconut.co.uk

CGP —
Coconut Gibbon Patrol
Working to keep your coconuts monkey-free

If you type a URL into the 'Address' box at the top of the page and hit 'Enter', you'll be taken straight to the website.

You Can Bookmark Your Favourite Sites

You can bookmark the websites that you use the most, so you can get to them more quickly. This adds them to the favourites list.

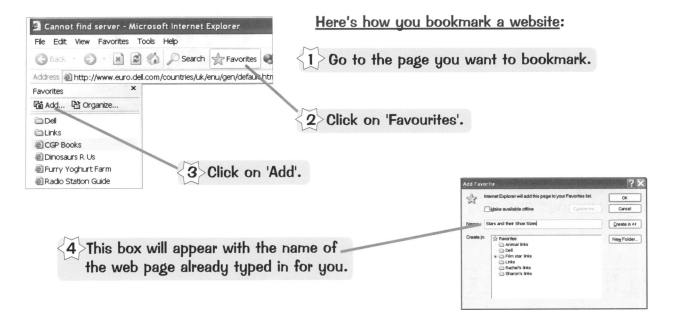

Here's how you bookmark a website:

1 Go to the page you want to bookmark.

2 Click on 'Favourites'.

3 Click on 'Add'.

4 This box will appear with the name of the web page already typed in for you.

5 Choose which folder you want to save it in and click OK.

To go to a website you've bookmarked, click on 'Favourites', then on the name of the website.

Bookmarking websites means you get to them fast...

If you type any of a URL wrong it won't work. That's why bookmarks are so useful — one click and you're there. If you need to create a new folder to store your bookmark in, it's easy. Click on 'New Folder' in the 'Add Favourite' box, then type in a name for the folder and click OK.

Copying and Pasting Stuff

You can Copy things from a Web Page and Paste them into Your Own Document

You can copy bits from the Internet (e.g. photos or bits of text) and paste them into a document (e.g. Word).

But see page 31 about copyright before you do this.

It's a lot easier than cutting and gluing bits of printed pages together.

Here's how you do it:

1 First, open up the document you want your copied bit to end up in.

2 Then get on the Internet and right-click on the thing you want to copy (like our logo, for example).

3 This menu will appear, so select 'Copy'.

4 Now go back into your document and then right-click anywhere on the page.

5 Then just click on 'Paste' and the copy will appear as if by magic. Or possibly ICT.

THE SAME GOES FOR TEXT — JUST REMEMBER TO HIGHLIGHT THE RIGHT BITS FIRST

You Won't Always Be Able To Copy Things

This doesn't always work. Sometimes all that will get copied is the URL, rather than the picture or piece of text you actually wanted.

There are lots of different reasons why this might happen — the main thing is that you'll need to copy something different.

It's OK to copy... It's OK to copy...

It looks really swanky if you copy and paste text and pictures from the Internet into your own documents. But only copy things that are relevant — don't just stick in loads of things because they look impressive. The copy and paste tools work in the same way as usual.

Using The Information

It's Useful to Print the Pages You Need

...just click on the 'Print' icon here.

The best bit about printing pages is that you can mark out the key bits of information for yourself with a pen.

Blah blah blah blah blah blah blah blah kind of like being able to highlight this bit blah blah blah blah blah blah blah blah blah...

Ask Before You Use Other People's Ideas

You can copy and paste things off the Internet, but you have to be careful because —

 YOU'RE NOT ALWAYS ALLOWED TO.

When someone has the copyright for a certain thing (a picture, a book, a piece of text or even an entire website) it means they own it and have control over how it's used.

If you use something that's owned by someone else without them knowing, it's like stealing and you can get in a lot of trouble. If you want to use something from a website, you have to ask for permission — but this can take ages.

> I asked Mr Freeze the ice-cream man if I could use his logo. He told me I could if I didn't say anything that made him look bad. I ended up not using the logo because I wanted to say that Mr Freeze made me vomit.

There is a way round this (sort of) —

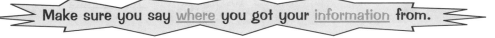 Make sure you say where you got your information from.

Oi — you haven't got the copyright on those sausages you mongrel...

If you do this, you can still use the information in your project.

Ask before you take — plain old good manners really...

People get really annoyed when other people use their things without asking — it's the same with the Internet. Someone might have spent a lifetime researching a topic, so for everything you use in your document, make sure you say who wrote it, rather than take credit for it yourself.

Organising Information

Information means things like phone numbers, dates and times.
Organising information means putting it in a sensible order.

It's Hard to Find Things in a Messy Pile

I've got all this information about monsters on bits of paper in a messy pile.

It takes ages to find out how many heads the monster 'Kar Dillak' has.

That's because my information is not organised.

Record Cards are a Way to Organise Facts

You can use record cards to organise information.
A record card is just a piece of card with information on it.

These record cards are about different monsters.

Each record card has information about one monster.

Name:	Peekoop
Lives in:	Trees and bushes
Number of Heads: 10	
Can fly:	Yes

To keep information about ten monsters, you need ten record cards.

Name:	Kar Dillak
Lives in:	Swamps
Number of Heads: 3	
Can fly:	No

Now it's easy to find information.
Kar Dillak has three heads.

The information is easy to find if the cards are kept in alphabetical order.

Record cards are better than piles (of paper)...

If you don't keep things organised, you're likely to be swamped by tatty bits of paper.
Putting information on record cards and keeping them in alphabetical order keeps the place tidy.
AND it makes it much quicker to find what you're looking for.

Records and Fields

Instead of saying 'record card', people often just say '<u>record</u>'.

Records are Split into Bits called Fields

Records have different <u>fields</u>.
A field contains <u>one</u> piece of information.

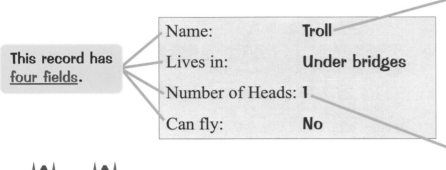

		This is the information in the '<u>Name</u>' field.
This record has <u>four fields</u>.	Name: **Troll**	
	Lives in: **Under bridges**	
	Number of Heads: **1**	
	Can fly: **No**	This is the information in the '<u>Number of Heads</u>' field.

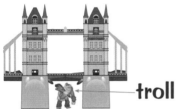

troll

There are Three Different Kinds of Field

Each field can have...

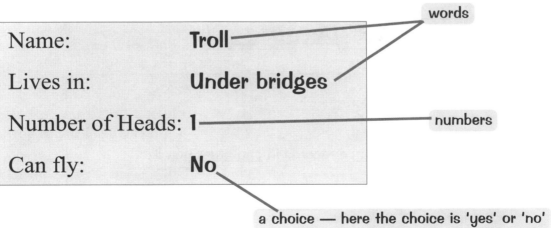

Name: **Troll** — words

Lives in: **Under bridges**

Number of Heads: **1** — numbers

Can fly: **No**

a choice — here the choice is 'yes' or 'no'

Farmers are organised — they've got lots of fields...

Remember that you break up information into records, and that you break up records into fields.
Confusing? Don't fret, all will become clear in the next few pages about databases.
Don't forget the 3 possible types of information held in a field — numbers, words or a choice.

Databases

Databases are like <u>record cards</u> on the <u>computer</u>. They can be really useful.

Databases *Organise Information* For You

Databases make it <u>easy</u> to organise information.
This database program is called <u>Junior Viewpoint</u>.

It even looks just like a <u>record card</u>.

Use these buttons to see the records of <u>different monsters</u>.

Use these buttons to go to the <u>first</u> or <u>last</u> record.

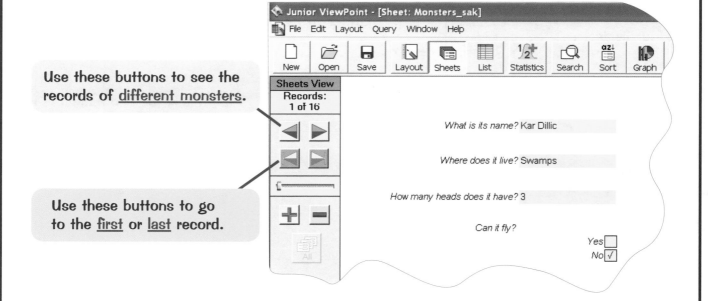

Databases *are* Great Because...

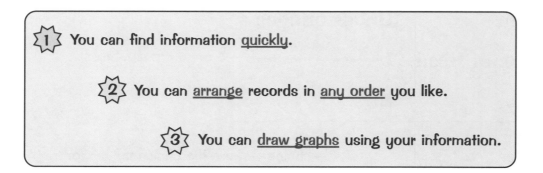

1 You can find information <u>quickly</u>.

2 You can <u>arrange</u> records in <u>any order</u> you like.

3 You can <u>draw graphs</u> using your information.

Relieve brain-strain — store information in databases...

This page tells you what a database is. Make sure you understand it, because the rest of this section tells you how to use them and what you can do with them.

Questionnaires

Information is much <u>easier to use</u> if you collect it in the <u>right way</u>.

A <u>Questionnaire</u> Makes Things Easier

If everyone writes their details in <u>different ways</u>, it's much <u>harder</u> to use the information in a database.

It's easier if everyone fills in a <u>standard sheet</u> that's the same for everyone.

Forms specially designed to <u>collect information</u> are called <u>questionnaires</u>.

You Can Use a <u>Computer</u> To Make Your <u>Questionnaires</u>

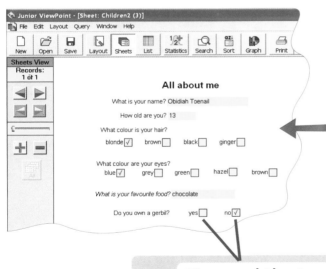

- You could use a <u>word processor</u> to make a questionnaire, but some <u>databases</u> let you make them too.

I made this one with Junior ViewPoint.

- You can <u>print out</u> copies of your questionnaire, or you can just fill it in <u>on the screen</u>.

It's a good idea to use <u>tick boxes</u> when there are only a few possible answers (e.g. like "yes" and "no").

Computers are <u>fast</u>, but they're <u>not as brainy</u> as you. We know that "yes", "YES", "Y" and "yep" all mean the same thing, but computers get <u>confused</u>.

This page will answer all your questions...

Questionnaires help you to get standard information that you can put into a database easily. Each question in the questionnaire is a <u>field</u>. You need to make sure that all the answers to a question give the same type of information (i.e. words, numbers or choice).

Adding and Sorting Information

It's Easy to Add Information to a Database

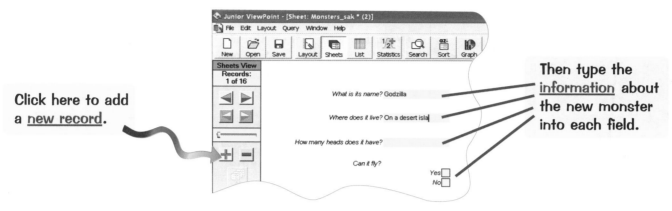

Click here to add a <u>new record</u>.

Then type the <u>information</u> about the new monster into each field.

Databases <u>aren't</u> all the same — sometimes the button to add new information looks a bit <u>different</u>. It could look like this:

You can Sort Your Database

It's easy to <u>sort</u> a database into <u>alphabetical order</u>.
You can also put <u>numbers in order</u> — smallest first, biggest last.

Here's how:

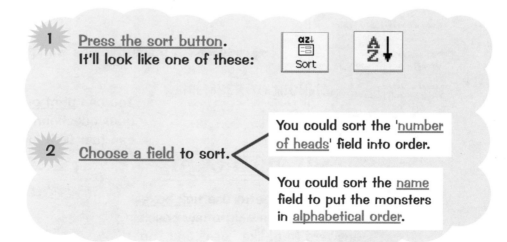

1 <u>Press the sort button</u>.
It'll look like one of these:

2 <u>Choose a field</u> to sort.

You could sort the '<u>number of heads</u>' field into order.

You could sort the <u>name</u> field to put the monsters in <u>alphabetical order</u>.

This makes it easy to <u>answer questions</u> like:
- Which monster has the <u>most heads</u>?
- How many monsters <u>can fly</u>?

Sort your life out — use a database...

Adding records is dead easy, but in some programs there isn't a shortcut button — instead you have to go to the 'Insert' menu and click on 'New Record'.

Searching Databases

You can find things in a database by doing a <u>search</u>.
You could <u>search</u> for all the people with <u>blue eyes</u>. It's easy.

Searching *a Database is* Easy

This is how you find all the people with <u>blue eyes</u>:

1 Press the <u>Search</u> button.
It'll look something like this.

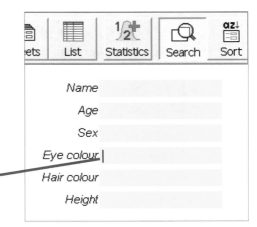

2 Choose the <u>field</u>. Here it'll be <u>Eye colour</u>.
You may have to <u>click on the field</u>
or <u>choose from a list</u> of fields.

In Junior Viewpoint you
click on the field.

3 <u>Type in</u> the eye colour you want to search for. Here it's "<u>blue</u>".

4 All the records for people with <u>blue eyes</u> will show up.

You can Search **for** Answers to Questions

<u>Searching</u> a database makes it easy to <u>answer questions</u> too.
You can answer questions like these:

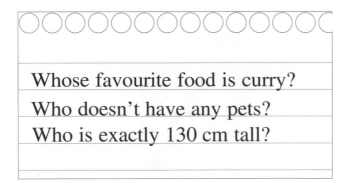

Whose favourite food is curry?
Who doesn't have any pets?
Who is exactly 130 cm tall?

Not another page on databases — change the record...

Using the search tool means that you get to the answer immediately, without having to do
any of the looking yourself — groovy.

Drawing Graphs

Charts and graphs are a great way to show <u>information</u>.
They're much <u>easier to read</u> than lots of numbers.

There are Three Main Types of Graph

BAR CHARTS

<u>Bar charts</u> are good for showing things that you want to <u>compare</u>. On this bar chart, it's easy to tell which TV sport is the <u>most</u> popular and which is the <u>least</u> popular.

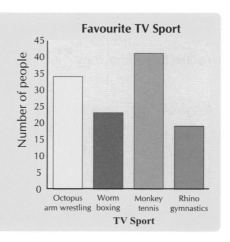

PIE CHARTS

<u>Pie charts</u> are great for showing <u>fractions</u> of things.

In this pie chart it's easy to tell that about a <u>quarter</u> of my friends enjoy parachute chess.

LINE GRAPHS

Line graphs are great for things which <u>change smoothly</u>, like <u>temperature</u> or someone's <u>height</u>.

You <u>never</u> see the temperature just <u>jump</u> from 10 °C to 20 °C — it goes through all the values in between.

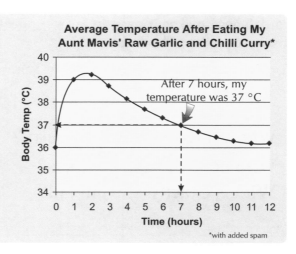

Bar, pie or line? — make sure you choose the right one...

Graphs are great for showing you lots of information in an easy-to-read way —
you can find something out in a second just by looking at a graph.

Drawing Graphs

You can use database programs to draw <u>charts</u> and <u>graphs</u>.
These make the information easier to read and <u>easier to interpret</u>.

Draw a <u>Graph</u> from a <u>Database</u> — It's <u>Easy</u>

1 Press the <u>Graph</u> button.

2 Choose which <u>fields</u> you want to use.

3 Choose the <u>type of graph</u> you want.

4 Hit the <u>Plot</u> button.

(Some databases will look a bit different from this, but they all work in a similar way.)

Make sure your <u>Charts and Graphs</u> are <u>Easy to Read</u>

When you draw a graph or chart, always give it a <u>title</u>.
If it has a title, then other people will know <u>what it shows</u>.

Always make
sure the <u>axes</u>
are <u>labelled</u>.

You can use different <u>colours</u> and <u>shades</u> to
make it <u>easier to read</u> (and less boring).

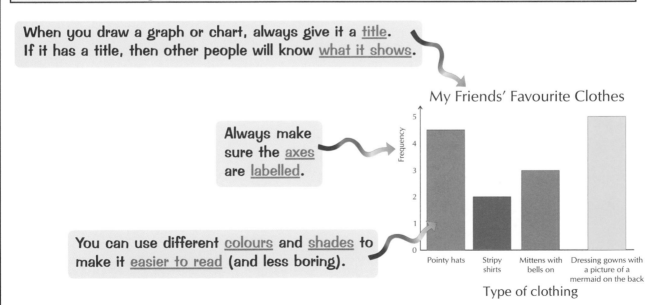

Give your graph a title — Sir Pie Chart...

Using graphs in database programs is really easy — all you have to do is say which fields you
want to be shown in the graph, and the database program does all the drawing for you.
But, it's up to you to add the finishing touches — adding labels and making it look pretty.

Tree Diagrams

You can use a tree diagram in science to identify plants and animals.
A <u>tree diagram</u> can also be called a <u>key</u>, a <u>branched key</u> or a <u>branching database</u>.

<u>You can use</u> Tree Diagrams <u>to</u> Identify Things

THE ALIENS:

<u>Follow these Steps To</u> Identify Each Alien

1) Start at the <u>top</u> of the tree diagram.
2) Ask yourself the <u>first question</u>.
   If the answer's '<u>YES</u>', follow the 'YES' line. If it's '<u>NO</u>', follow the 'NO' line.
3) Ask yourself the <u>next question</u>.
   If the answer's '<u>YES</u>', follow the 'YES' line. If it's '<u>NO</u>', follow the 'NO' line.
4) <u>Keep going</u> till you get an answer.
5) <u>Write</u> it down.

THE TREE DIAGRAM:

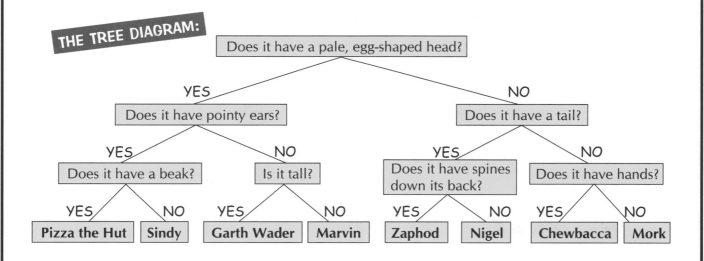

<u>Tree diagrams are as easy as one, two, tree...</u>

They're called tree diagrams because they kind of look like trees when you draw them out.
E.g. the first question is like the trunk, the next 2 are like big branches, the next 4 are smaller
branches etc, and the last questions are like twigs. OK, so it takes a bit of imagination...

Shapes of Tree Diagrams

Some Tree Diagrams get to the Answer *Slowly*

Here's a tree diagram of 8 animals.

1) To identify the penguin, you need to ask just <u>2 questions</u>.

2) But to identify the cat or the ape, you need to ask <u>5 questions</u>.

3) It's <u>not a very good tree diagram</u> — there are only <u>8 animals</u>, but you sometimes have to ask <u>5 questions</u> to get to the bottom.

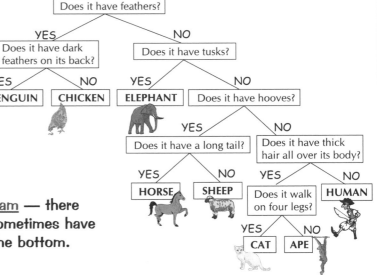

Some Tree Diagrams get the Answer *Quickly*

1) This is <u>a better tree diagram</u> of the same animals.

2) You can identify <u>any</u> animal by asking just <u>3 questions</u>.

3) Each question splits the remaining animals into 2 <u>equally-sized</u> groups.

4) Tree diagrams work <u>much better</u> that way.

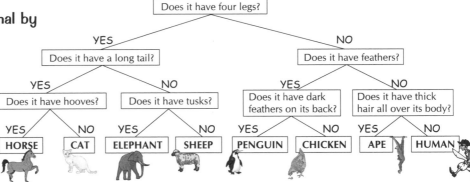

GOOD QUESTIONS SPLIT THE GROUP IN HALF

Halve the group to double your success...

Think carefully about the questions you ask in a tree diagram — wherever possible ask questions that will split the group in 2 so that you'll definitely get rid of half the group each time.
If your 'tree' looks lopsided at the end, then it's a fair bet that your questions aren't good ones.

Branching Databases

You can do <u>tree diagrams</u> on a computer — they're called "<u>branching databases</u>".

Here's how to Create a Branching Database

Whatever program you've got, follow these steps:

1) You start by typing in a <u>list of things</u>.

2) Then you type in a question that'll split the group roughly <u>in half</u>.

3) Answer that question about <u>everything</u> in your group.

4) The computer uses your answers to put the things into <u>two groups</u>.

5) For each of the smaller groups you need to think of <u>another question</u> to split it in half.

6) You keep doing this till <u>all</u> the groups are <u>split up</u> and you've just got <u>answers</u>.

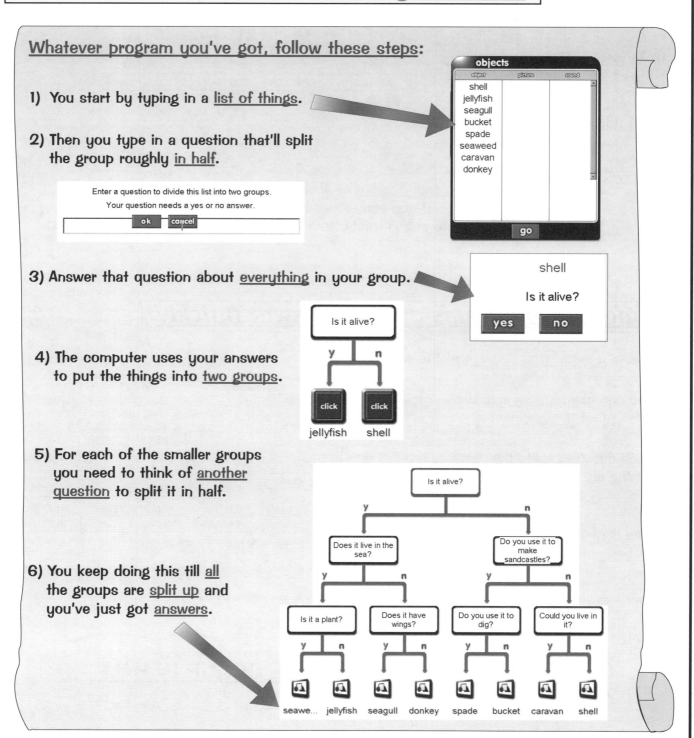

Branch out and use a database for tree diagrams...

It's easier to use a database program to draw tree diagrams, but <u>you</u> still have to think of the questions. Possible database programs that you might use include Granada Branch, Primary Trees and Branches, BlackCat Decisions and Textease Branch — they all do very similar things.

Section Five — Using Databases

Doing Database Searches

You can search a database for <u>words or numbers</u>. It's also really easy
to search for numbers which are <u>bigger or smaller</u> than a certain number.

Searching Databases is Easy

1 Press the <u>search</u> button:

2 Choose a <u>field</u> to search.

3 Type a <u>word</u> or <u>number</u> to search for.

Use > and < for Greater Than and Less Than

< means "less than"	<= means "less than and including"
> means "greater than"	>= means "greater than and including"

(On some programs, you have to put => or =< instead of >= and <=)

EXAMPLE: Which planets and moons are smaller than the Earth?

1 I need to search the <u>Diameter</u> field
because diameter is a measure of <u>size</u>.

2 The Earth's diameter is <u>12756 km</u>.
So I need to search for "<u><12756</u>".

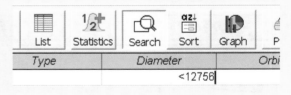

EXAMPLE: Which planets have 2 or more moons?

1 The field is easy this time,
it's the <u>Moons</u> field.

2 I need to search for "<u>>= 2</u>" which
means "<u>greater than and including 2</u>".

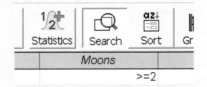

Could anything be greater than this page?...

These mathematical symbols are only useful for number searches. Don't be put off by them —
they make your life easier, and mean you don't have to write out long sentences in every search.

AND and OR Searches

If you want to do really clever searches, you'll need to use the search words <u>AND</u> and <u>OR</u>.

AND *Finds When Two Things Are True*

EXAMPLE: Find planets and moons which are warmer than -50°C, but colder than 100°C?

 The <u>Temp</u> field shows the surface temperature.

 The temperature needs to be greater than -50 °C <u>AND</u> less than 100 °C

Atmosphere	Temp
	>-50 AND <100

 So the search is **> –50 AND < 100**.

 And it goes in the <u>Temp</u> field.

There are <u>2 matches</u> — Earth and Mars.

Chosen by:Temp >-50 AND <100

Name	Temp	Atmosph
Earth	15	77% nitrogi
Mars	-23	Carbon dio

Tad hot, this planet.

OR *Finds When Either Thing Is True*

EXAMPLE: Find all the moons that orbit Mars or Pluto.

 You need to search the <u>Orbits</u> field.

 So type the search **Mars OR Pluto** into the Orbits field.

There are <u>3 matches</u>:
Mars has <u>two moons</u> called Phobos and Deimos.
Pluto has <u>one moon</u> called Charon.

AND/OR — *two tiny words that are a big help...*

AND and OR search words both help you narrow down your search even more, so you get to the right answer more quickly. It makes sense really — just think how you would ask in real life. E.g. Who has sandwiches <u>and</u> crisps for lunch? / Who is playing football <u>or</u> tennis tonight?

Searching the Internet

The <u>Internet</u> is a bit like a database. A really, really <u>huge one</u>.

Use 'Search Engines' to find stuff on the Internet

<u>Search engines</u> are the best way to find stuff on the Internet.

I want to find out about Birmingham,
so I type <u>Birmingham</u> and press <u>Search</u>.

EEK! — Most of the websites it has found are about Birmingham in <u>America</u>!

AND and OR searches work on the Internet

I'm going to try an <u>AND</u> search to find websites about Birmingham in the UK.

AH, THAT'S BETTER — Now all the websites are about the UK Birmingham.

There's loads of information on the Internet, but...

1 You often have to do lots of different searches before you find what you want.

2 Anyone can make a website, so don't trust everything that you find.

Ask yourself some searching questions...

Internet searches are used for loads of things these days — business, school work, academic research, for fun, etc — so it's important that you learn how to use search engines well.
Look back over pages 26 and 27 for more stuff on how to do good Internet searches.

Testing Ideas

You can turn your database results into graphs to test predictions.

Graphs Let You See If Your Predictions Are Right...

I've got a few ideas about birds, but I'm not sure if they're right.
I'm going to use a bird database to find out if my ideas are correct.

Birds
Name goshawk
Lives large trees
Eats small birds/mammals
Length (in cm) 55
Wingspan (in cm) 150
Number of eggs 3

MY PREDICTION:

I think that longer birds will usually have bigger wingspans than shorter birds.

I can test this prediction by making the database draw a scatter graph of length of bird against wingspan.

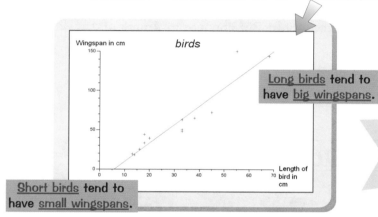

Long birds tend to have big wingspans.

Short birds tend to have small wingspans.

The graph shows that longer birds nearly always have bigger wingspans. This means my prediction is right.

...Or if They're Wrong

MY OTHER PREDICTION:

I think that birds with bigger wingspans will lay more eggs.

I can test this by drawing a scatter graph of wingspan against number of eggs.

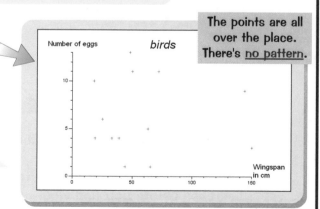

The points are all over the place. There's no pattern.

The graph shows that the number of eggs a bird lays has nothing to do with wingspan. My prediction is wrong.

I predict a cucumber invasion — but I may be wrong...

It's hard to use databases to test predictions just by looking at all the separate records.
Instead, you have to put the information together in graphs, so that you can see patterns clearly.

Section Six — Analysing Data

Database Accuracy

When <u>mistakes</u> happen in <u>real-life databases</u>, they can cause some <u>nasty problems</u>...

Even Simple Mistakes in Databases Cause Problems

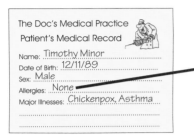

The Doc's Medical Practice
Patient's Medical Record
Name: Timothy Minor
Date of Birth: 12/11/89
Sex: Male
Allergies: None
Major Illnesses: Chickenpox, Asthma

Timothy has hayfever, but his <u>doctor</u> hasn't written it down. So Timothy has no tablets and a runny nose.

And <u>police</u> databases — if the wrong name was entered for a crime, you could have a criminal record and not know it!

<u>Banks</u> use databases — mistakes could mean they think you have no money when actually you're loaded.

Information on the Internet might NOT be Accurate

<u>Anyone</u> can put information on the Internet, and there's no one to <u>check</u> that it's correct.

Some information is <u>biased</u>, i.e. it's <u>for</u> or <u>against</u> something.

Here are some <u>biased sites</u>:

 1 My mate Eleanor thinks the Earth is flat. She's even made a website about it.

Eleanor's Flat Earth Website

The Earth is flat like this.

CGP

The Fastest Car Ever...

...is my dad's. It's really fast.

CGP

 2 This is Brian's website — he reckons his dad's car is the fastest in the world. I searched the Internet for the fastest car, and Brian's dad's came up.

Pesky humans — always making mistakes...

No matter how useful databases are, they still need information putting into them by humans, and humans make mistakes quite often. It's up to you to spot the errors when you use them.

Checking for Accuracy

Errors can crop up quite a lot in databases, which causes all kinds of problems.

There are THREE Main Types of Error

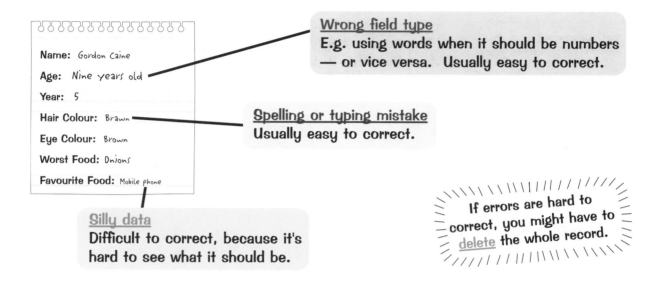

Name: Gordon Caine
Age: Nine years old
Year: 5
Hair Colour: Brawn
Eye Colour: Brown
Worst Food: Onions
Favourite Food: Mobile phone

Wrong field type
E.g. using words when it should be numbers — or vice versa. Usually easy to correct.

Spelling or typing mistake
Usually easy to correct.

Silly data
Difficult to correct, because it's hard to see what it should be.

If errors are hard to correct, you might have to delete the whole record.

Different Errors Cause Different Problems

Below is a train timetable with an error in it.

From	To	Departure Time	Arrival Time
Ulverston	Foxfield	11.18	12.06
Ulverston	Foxfield	13.36	14.23
Ulverston	Foxfield	16.04	16.55
Ulverston	Foxfield	14.18	19.06
Foxfield	Ulverston	9.09	9.58
Foxfield	Ulverston	11.22	12.11
Foxfield	Ulverston	13.46	14.32
Foxfield	Ulverston	19.43	20.36

This is a typing mistake. It should probably be 18:18.

This timetable error could mean:
1. People won't know there is a train at 18:18.
2. People might try to catch the non-existent 14:18 train.
3. People might not go to Ulverston because there's no evening train back.

Everyone makes mistakes — exsept me of course...

Usually you can spot errors in databases and alter them, but sometimes you can't work out what's supposed to be written so you have to delete the record. Different errors cause different problems, e.g. money problems in a bank database, transport problems in a timetable database.

Checking for Accuracy Using Graphs

Errors can be really Hard to Spot

The table below shows Brian's height on different birthdays.

Brian's Birthday Height Chart

Birthday (in years)	1	2	3	4	5	6	7	8	9	10	11	12	13
Height (in cm)	75.6	91.4	99.0	106.7	111.8	102.7	124.5	129.5	135.3	140.3	145.4	149.9	154.9

There's an error in it — but it's hard to spot.

Drawing a Graph Can Help You See Errors More Easily

This <u>line graph</u> of the table above makes it much easier to spot the error.

Any kink in the line could be an error.

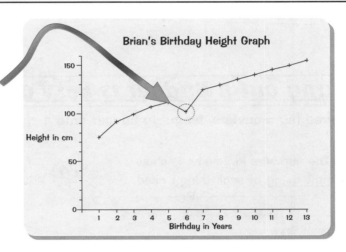

Line Graphs are for Continuous Data

Line graphs should only be used for <u>continuous data</u>.
Continuous data changes <u>smoothly</u>, like temperature or height. People don't suddenly jump from 140 cm to 155 cm — they grow through all the values in between.

If you used a bar chart, it would look <u>silly</u> — as if people suddenly became bigger.

Learn how to catch fishy data...

It's hard to detect patterns from lists of numbers — it's only when the numbers are put into a graph that you can identify possible errors. Look out for any bits of the graph that look odd, and double check for errors there. Remember to use the right kind of graph to display results.

Budgets

Budgets show how someone plans to spend money.

Budgets are Lists of Things You Need to Buy

I've invited some monsters round for tea. I have £42 to spend on food and drink.
This is my budget:

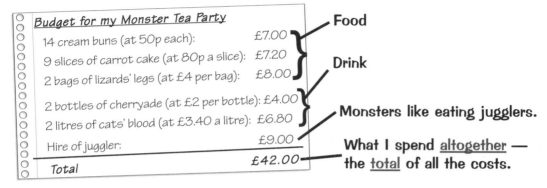

Budget for my Monster Tea Party

14 cream buns (at 50p each):	£7.00
9 slices of carrot cake (at 80p a slice):	£7.20
2 bags of lizards' legs (at £4 per bag):	£8.00
2 bottles of cherryade (at £2 per bottle):	£4.00
2 litres of cats' blood (at £3.40 a litre):	£6.80
Hire of juggler:	£9.00
Total	£42.00

Food

Drink

Monsters like eating jugglers.

What I spend altogether — the total of all the costs.

Working out a Budget is Easy on a Spreadsheet

I've entered my monsters' tea party budget onto a spreadsheet.

1 The numbers in column D show how many of each thing I need...

2 ...Column E shows the price of 1 item...

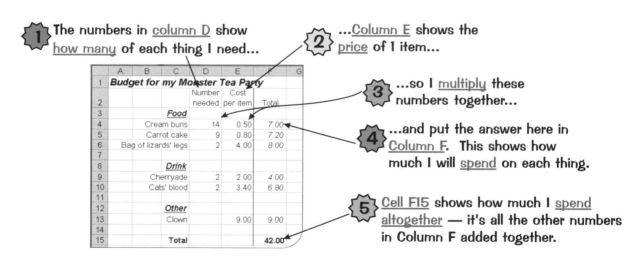

	A	B	C	D	E	F	G
1	*Budget for my Monster Tea Party*						
2				Number needed	Cost per item	Total	
3			*Food*				
4		Cream buns		14	0.50	7.00	
5		Carrot cake		9	0.80	7.20	
6		Bag of lizards' legs		2	4.00	8.00	
7							
8			*Drink*				
9		Cherryade		2	2.00	4.00	
10		Cats' blood		2	3.40	6.80	
11							
12			*Other*				
13		Clown			9.00	9.00	
14							
15			Total			42.00	

3 ...so I multiply these numbers together...

4 ...and put the answer here in Column F. This shows how much I will spend on each thing.

5 Cell F15 shows how much I spend altogether — it's all the other numbers in Column F added together.

Computers are Great for Budgets

There are two main reasons why computers are great for doing budgets on:

 1   Computers can calculate things really quickly.

 2   You can change your budget and see the effects straight away.

Don't bodge it when you budget — use spreadsheets...

Working out a budget takes a long time, but if you do it on a spreadsheet it's much quicker
because the computer does all the calculations for you. It's extra handy for when you have
to change something in your budget (e.g. if the price of something goes up).

Spreadsheets

Spreadsheets are fantastic for doing calculations.

Spreadsheets Have Loads of Cells

A spreadsheet has lots of boxes arranged in rows and columns. Each box is called a cell.

Cells are described using letters and numbers.

This is cell A4...

...and this is cell B5.

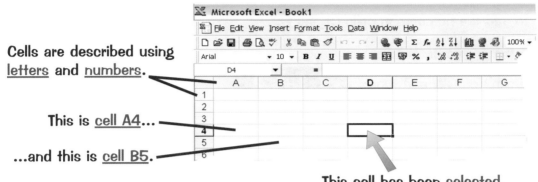

This cell has been selected. If you type something, it will appear here.

Use the arrow keys to move from cell to cell. Or just click in a cell using the mouse.

Adjust the Rows and Columns

I've made a spreadsheet of my friends' hobbies, but some of the columns are too narrow.

1 Columns B and C are too narrow — you can't read all the information.

2 If I move the cursor halfway between the two letters, it changes shape...

3 ...and I can change the column width by dragging it.

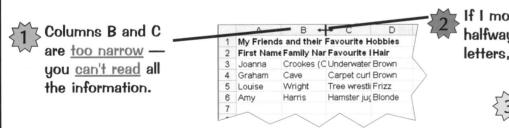

It's much better like this:

Spreadsheets are evil — they put things in cells...

Spreadsheets are really useful, and they're easy to use too. There are loads of tricks you can use to make the cells look like you want them to, such as adding colour or thick borders.
Tip: — double-click between column labels — the columns should become the perfect size.

Formulas

Let the spreadsheet know you want it to calculate something by writing a <u>formula</u>.

Enter Formulas Using an *Equals Sign*

A formula always starts with an <u>equals sign</u> (=).

- I want to <u>add</u> the numbers in cells <u>C1 and C2</u>.

  - I want the <u>answer</u> in cell <u>C3</u>.

    - So I <u>click</u> on <u>C3</u>, and type: **=C1+C2**

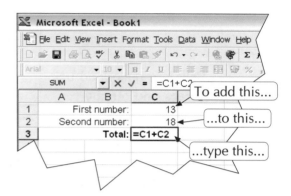

You can do more than just add...
Try these lovely formulas:

=C1–C2	=C1/C2	=C1*C2
(subtract)	(divide)	(multiply)

Instead of typing 'C1', I can just <u>click on the cell</u>. The computer writes 'C1' in my formula <u>automatically</u>.

Change What's in a Cell Using the *Formula Bar*

<u>Changing</u> what's in a cell is easy. You can change numbers, text or formulas.

 Click on a cell — its contents appear in the <u>formula bar</u>.

 <u>Click</u> in the formula bar and change things in the <u>normal way</u>.

 Press '<u>Enter</u>' when you finish.

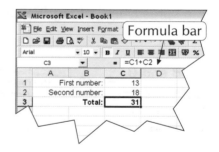

To see what formula is in a cell, click on it and look in the formula bar.

Spreadsheets Change Answers *Automatically*

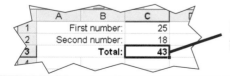

If I <u>change the number</u> in cell C1 to 25, the <u>answer</u> in cell C3 changes <u>automatically</u> — like magic.

This page contains the secret formula for ICT success...

Spreadsheet formulas can seem a bit tricky to begin with, but they're worth learning — once you've got the hang of writing them, you'll be laughing. They make calculations really easy and quick, with minimum effort on your part. If only everything in life was so simple...

Formulas

Spreadsheets can do a lot more than add two numbers together.

Use SUM to Add Lots of Numbers Together

I want to find out how much faffing about I've done today.

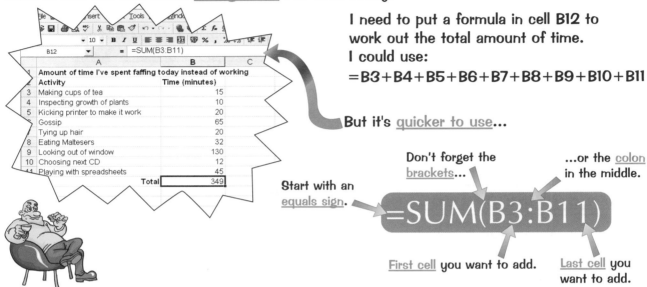

I need to put a formula in cell B12 to work out the total amount of time.
I could use:

=B3+B4+B5+B6+B7+B8+B9+B10+B11

But it's quicker to use...

Don't forget the brackets...   ...or the colon in the middle.

Start with an equals sign.

=SUM(B3:B11)

First cell you want to add.   Last cell you want to add.

Sometimes you Need Loads of Formulas

This is a multiplication table. The third column multiplies the numbers in the first two columns.

	A	B	C
1	Number A	Number B	Number A × Number B
2	4	1	
3	4	2	
4	4	3	
5	4	4	

I need to put the formula "=A2*B2" in cell C2...

... and put formulas in all the other cells like this:

=A3*B3

=A4*B4 etc

I can do this loads quicker by using 'Copy' and 'Paste'.

 1 Type in the first formula (=A2*B2).

2 Then copy and paste it to the next cell. The computer changes the formula when I paste it. It puts =A4*B4 into cell C4, puts =A5*B5 into C5 and so on.

	A	B	C
1	Number A	Number B	Number A × Number B
2	4	1	=A2*B2
3	4	2	
4	4	3	
5	4	4	
6	4	5	

copy and paste
...and paste
...and paste

3 To complete the table, just keep pasting all the way down.

Using SUM adds up to less work for you...

Using SUM is great — it's quick, and you're less likely to make mistakes. Copy and paste is also useful — a handy tip is to paste all the cells in one go. Copy the first cell, select all the cells you want to paste into and then paste — you can do a whole column in one go like this.

Maths with Spreadsheets

Another thing that spreadsheets are good for is... well, urr ...maths.

A Quick Reminder of some Easy Maths

You probably already know these rectangle formulas, but if you've forgotten...

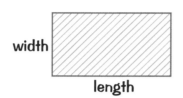

width

length

Area is the amount of space a shape takes up.
The area of a rectangle is the length × width.

Perimeter is the distance round the outside of a shape.
The perimeter of a rectangle is 2 × (length + width).

You can use Spreadsheets like Calculators

I've made a spreadsheet to calculate the area and perimeter of any rectangle.

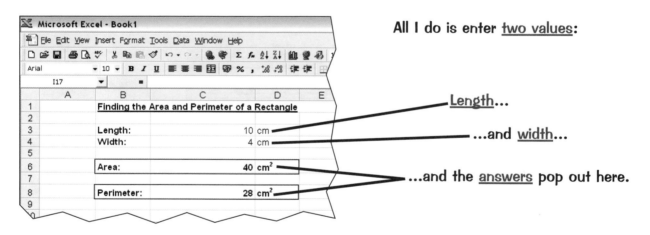

All I do is enter two values:

Length...

...and width...

...and the answers pop out here.

If I change the length or width value, the area and perimeter change automatically. It's magic.

Formulas are the Secret

This spreadsheet uses two formulas —
one to calculate area and one to calculate perimeter.

 1 The area formula is =C3*C4 and goes in cell C6.

 2 The perimeter formula is = 2*(C3 + C4) and goes in cell C8.

Maths, yuk — but never fear, spreadsheets are here...

Once you've set up the formulas in a spreadsheet, you can use it like a calculator — cool, huh. All you do is put in the right figures and the computer does all the number-crunching, brain-power stuff. If technology continues like this, one day we won't need brains at all...

Creating Graphs

Make a Graph from a Spreadsheet

Computers can plot points on a graph using numbers from a spreadsheet table.
The instructions below are for Microsoft Excel but the basic steps are the same in any program.

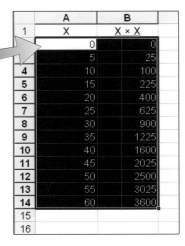

 Highlight the two columns of numbers in the table. *Click on cell A2 and, holding the mouse button down, drag the cursor down to B14.*

 Click the new chart button ( ).

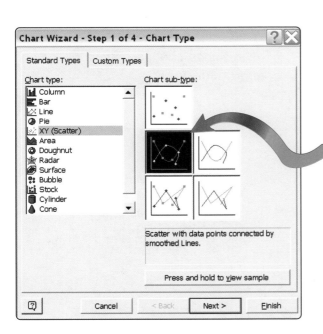

3 Choose the type of graph. Scatter graphs are best for plotting points, so choose the XY (Scatter) option and then pick this one. (It joins up all the points with a nice smooth line.)

 You'll need to choose a title and label for your graph. Your final graph should look something like this:

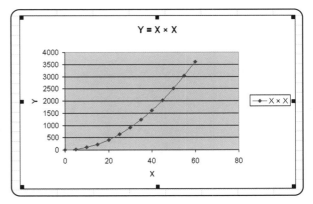

Plot to succeed — learn how to make graphs...

It's good to use spreadsheets to draw graphs — it's quick and accurate, and likely to be neater than a hand-drawn graph. Don't forget that there are loads of different types of graphs and charts you can make, e.g. bar charts, line graphs, mmmm... pie charts...

What are Simulations?

Simulation is a big word. It means "pretend".
With simulations you can pretend to fly a plane or ride a motorbike — on the computer.

There are Different Kinds of Simulation

Simulations are great — they let you try impossible things, train pilots and test new inventions.

A Virtual Pet (like a Tamagotchi).

Mjaaoowwww...

You can choose:
• what to feed them
• how often to play with them
• how often to clean the cage

These things change how happy your pet is.

A Flight Simulator

You can choose:
• how fast to fly
• how much to turn
• how high to fly

These things change how well you fly.

In most simulations you have to make choices. Your choices affect what happens.

An Adventure Game

The wizard fires a bolt of fire. Do you:
A: speak to him
B: run past him
C: run backwards

CGP

You can choose:
• which way to go
• which sword to use in a fight
• who to speak to

These things change how quickly you solve the puzzle, or how long you survive.

Need stimulation? — try a simulation...

Simulations are a really cool in a space-age kinda way — they let us do things that we otherwise wouldn't be able to experience. But there are problems with them — they are often too simple and they can be very expensive.

Finding Patterns

You Can Work Out What Difference Each Choice Makes

This page is about working out what <u>difference</u> each choice makes.

EXAMPLE: I kept four virtual plants for a month.
I gave each plant <u>different amounts of water</u>.

Do a <u>fair test</u> — only change <u>one</u> thing at a time.

Plant	How often I watered it	How tall it grew
A	not at all	10 cm
B	once a week	15 cm
C	once a day	25 cm
D	twice a day	30 cm

The Pattern:

The <u>more often</u> I <u>watered</u> a plant, the <u>taller</u> it <u>grew</u>.

Look at What's Happened Before

<u>Always</u> write down what you did and what happened — it makes it easier to <u>see patterns</u>.

Look at what happened <u>last time</u>. It'll probably happen <u>next time</u>.

EXAMPLE: My virtual dog usually <u>wags his tail</u> when I play with him.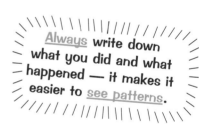

I think he will wag his tail <u>next time</u> I play with him

TEST IT OUT:

Looks like I <u>guessed right</u>...

Here's a pattern — whenever I tell a joke people moan...

You can work out how different choices affect what happens in a simulation. Do a fair test by only changing one thing at a time and by repeating the experiment to see if you got the same results. Then write down what happens, make a prediction from it, and test it out — no probs.

The Floor Turtle

A floor turtle is a <u>little robot</u> which carries a <u>pen</u>.
You can use it to <u>draw lines or shapes</u> on a piece of paper.

The Floor Turtle is a Little Robot

You control the turtle with these <u>commands</u>:

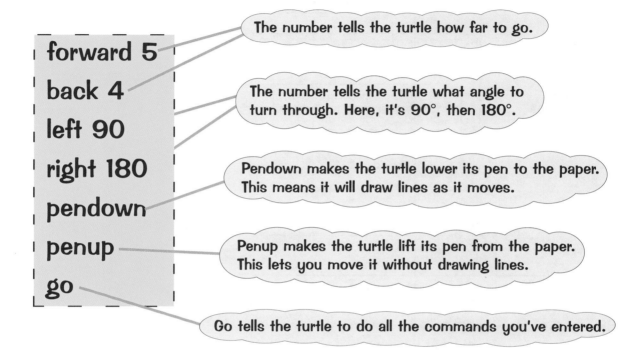

forward 5 — The number tells the turtle how far to go.

back 4

left 90 — The number tells the turtle what angle to turn through. Here, it's 90°, then 180°.

right 180

pendown — Pendown makes the turtle lower its pen to the paper. This means it will draw lines as it moves.

penup — Penup makes the turtle lift its pen from the paper. This lets you move it without drawing lines.

go — Go tells the turtle to do all the commands you've entered.

Watch the Turtle Follow this Sequence...

I'm afraid my floor turtle is broken (I dropped a fridge on it).
So my pet turtle, Toby, will <u>demonstrate</u> how the floor turtle works.

<u>SEQUENCE</u>:

pendown   forward 3   right 90   forward 5   left 90   forward 6

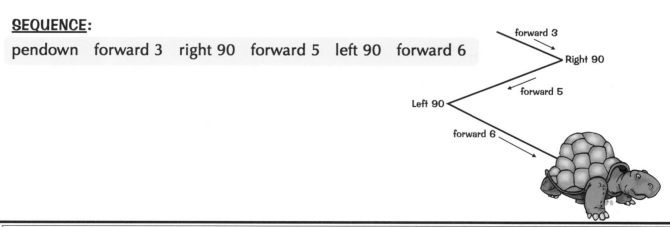

Seems like a hard way to draw a line...

OK, so it might seem a bit ridiculous to use commands to make a robot turtle draw lines onto a piece of paper, when you could draw it yourself in a couple of seconds... But, the point here is that you can use commands to create your own effect — so you're in charge of decisions.

Using LOGO

From now on, we're going to use a <u>computer</u> turtle instead of a floor turtle.
You use a "<u>LOGO</u>" program to do this.

LOGO is a *Computer Language*

LOGO is a <u>computer programming language</u>. It lets you move a "<u>turtle</u>" around the computer screen using the <u>same commands</u> as the floor turtle.

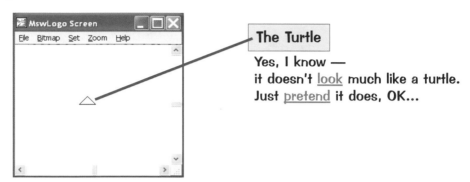

The Turtle

Yes, I know —
it doesn't <u>look</u> much like a turtle.
Just <u>pretend</u> it does, OK...

Type the commands here.

The turtle follows the command each time you press <u>Enter</u> (or <u>Execute</u>).

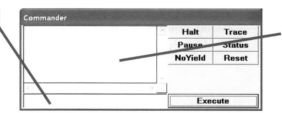

The commands you've already done are shown <u>here</u>.

Use the *Same Commands* as the *Floor Turtle*

If you've used the <u>floor turtle</u>, you'll find LOGO <u>really easy</u> to get started with.
Here it is in action:

forward 100
left 90
forward 200...

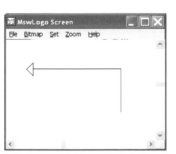

...right 80
 back 100...

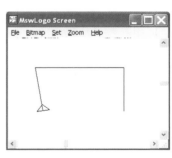

"CLEAR" AND "HOME" ARE REALLY USEFUL COMMANDS

"<u>Home</u>" puts the turtle back where it started (so it makes a loop).

"<u>Clear</u>" wipes the screen. (sometimes it's called <u>clean</u>)

LOGO does what you command — instant power-trip...

The LOGO commands are the same as for the floor turtle, but you use <u>bigger numbers</u> to move the turtle — e.g. use 'forward 50', instead of 'forward 3'. Also, be careful with spaces — e.g. 'forward50' won't work but 'forward 50' will, and 'penup' and 'pendown' don't have spaces.

Section Eight — Simulations

Repeating Things

It can get really annoying when you have to type in the same thing again and again.

The REPEAT Command is Great

We can draw a square by writing out each separate command:

> forward 50, right 90, forward 50, right 90,
> forward 50, right 90, forward 50, right 90.

But this way is a pain because you're typing the same two commands again and again. A much better way to do it is with the repeat command.

repeat 4 [forward 50 right 90]

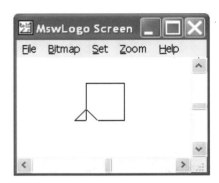

This says "repeat the bit in brackets 4 times".

Result — a lovely square,
with far less typing, hurray!

REPEAT Lets You Do Shapes Really Easily

It's easy to make shapes with any number of sides:

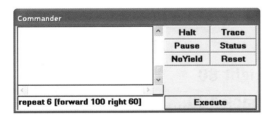

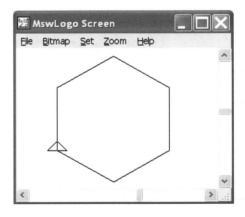

This gives a 6-sided shape (hexagon).
That's because the bit in brackets draws
one side and you repeat this 6 times.

> To make a shape join up, you need to turn through 360° in total
> (a full circle). Here, it turns 60° six times, because 6 × 60 = 360°.

I'll say this only once — REPEAT saves loads of effort...

Learn how to repeat commands, and you'll save yourself loads of aching wrists from typing in the future. Even if you wanted to draw a shape with 300 sides, you'd still only have to write one line of commands (as long as all the sides are the same).

Procedures

This page is about <u>procedures</u>. Don't worry, it's not as hard as it sounds.

You Can *Teach* The Computer *New Words*

You can use <u>procedures</u> to "teach" the computer how to do something.
You write a set of commands — a <u>procedure</u> — and give it a <u>name</u>.
Then when you type in that name, the turtle follows those commands.

I've taught the computer three new words — <u>ted</u>, <u>jack</u> and <u>dougal</u>.

Now, when I type <u>ted</u>...

...the turtle draws a <u>triangle</u>.

And <u>jack</u>...

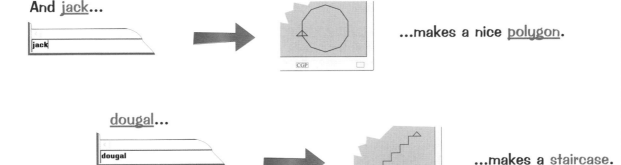

...makes a nice <u>polygon</u>.

<u>dougal</u>...

...makes a <u>staircase</u>.

Use The *New Word* Whenever You Like

When you've taught the computer a new word, you can use it <u>whenever you like</u>.

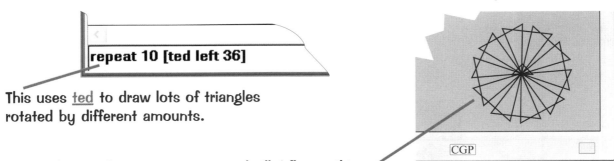

repeat 10 [ted left 36]

This uses <u>ted</u> to draw lots of triangles rotated by different amounts.

The result is an <u>amazing</u> windmill / flower thing.
And it only took <u>one</u> line of LOGO. If that doesn't excite you, I'm a poodle.

You can teach an old turtle new tricks...

In LOGO you can create your own set of commands and give it a name, so whenever you type that name, the computer follows that set of commands — which saves you the job of writing them out. It's dead handy for when you need to draw a particular shape a lot.

Monitoring

Machines can <u>monitor</u> things like <u>temperature</u>, <u>noise levels</u>, <u>sound levels</u> and so on.
This is useful in loads of different ways.

Monitoring Happens *Every Day*

<u>Weather forecasters</u> need loads of <u>accurate</u> information —
e.g. temperatures and wind speeds.

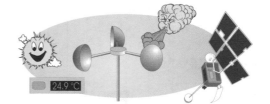

1 They need a lot of <u>measurements</u>
from <u>different places</u>.

Machines are used, which <u>automatically</u>
take measurements at regular intervals.

  2 Central heating in houses uses a <u>thermostat</u>
that monitors a room's temperature.

If the <u>temperature gets too low</u>, the heating is <u>turned on</u>.
If the <u>temperature gets too high</u>, the heating is <u>turned off</u>.

Anything that actually measures something is called a <u>sensor</u>.

Machines **Can Monitor Where** *People Can't*

 This could be because the measurements are
needed from places that are <u>hard to get to</u>.

Or because they are needed
over a very <u>short period</u>...

> Like the light levels during an
> explosion — measuring these
> could be dangerous as well.

 ...or over a very <u>long period</u>.

> Like outside temperatures —
> important for weather forecasting.

A mood monitor — now that'd be a great invention...

Monitoring is part of everyday life. Everyone takes it for granted that we know what the
weather is going to be like each week, but if it wasn't for monitoring, you wouldn't have a
clue — people would be wearing snowshoes in heatwaves and bikinis during blizzards.

Using Sensors

Computers are great for showing results. But the thing that actually measures things is called a sensor. You can attach sensors to a computer.

You can Attach Sensors to a Computer

Different sensors measure different things (e.g. sound levels or light levels). You can attach more than one sensor to a computer at a time.

The sensors might be attached to a sensor unit that you plug into the computer.

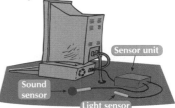

Results Can be Displayed in Different Ways

When you've attached a sensor to a computer, it's easy to display the results. I'm using Data Harvest software called 'Meters' and 'Graph', but other software is pretty similar.

 This is how the program 'Meters' displays results.
It shows what the readings from the sensors are now.

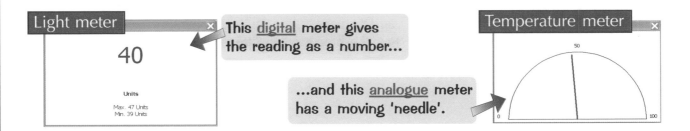

This digital meter gives the reading as a number...

...and this analogue meter has a moving 'needle'.

This is how the program 'Graph' shows the readings from a sensor. You can see how things have changed by plotting a graph.

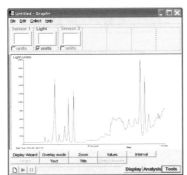

'Graph' is a more useful program than 'Meters', as it lets you collect data over a period of time.

(See P. 64 for more on how to use 'Graph'.)

Learn all this stuff — and get a sensor achievement

There are loads of different types of sensor that can be attached to computers — they measure all kinds of things like light, movement, temperature, sound, wind speed, rainfall. Showing the results in a graph means that you can look at changes and patterns over time.

Datalogging

Datalogging means <u>measuring</u> something over a period of time and <u>recording</u> the results.

Use 'Graph' for Datalogging

For datalogging, you need a program that can record results <u>over time</u> — like Data Harvest '<u>Graph</u>'. Other programs will work in a similar way.

1) Click on the '<u>New</u>' button to record new data ( ).

2) Select '<u>Real time</u>' in the window that pops up.

3) Select <u>how long</u> you want to collect data for. (Click '<u>Continuous</u>' if you want to collect data until you press the 'Stop' button.)

4) This is <u>how often</u> a reading will be taken...

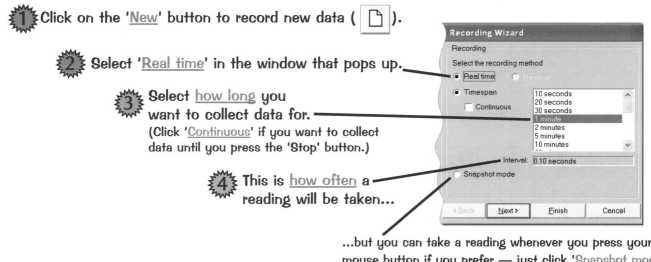

...but you can take a reading whenever you press your mouse button if you prefer — just click '<u>Snapshot mode</u>'.

5) Then select which <u>sensors</u> you want to use. Just tick the boxes on the left.

6) Now press the '<u>Start</u>' button and your results will appear while you watch.

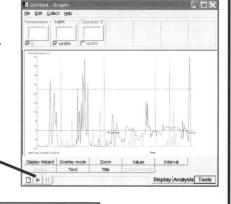

Sensors Can be Used Away From the Computer

1) <u>Click on 'Remote</u>' instead of 'Real time'.

2) <u>Unplug</u> your datalogger or sensor unit and take it away to do your recording.

3) When you get back, <u>reconnect</u> your datalogger or sensor unit to your computer and click on '<u>Collect Remote Data</u>'.

Datalogging — not a kind of forestry...

If you're recording something that changes slowly, it's a good idea to take measurements over a long period of time. And if something's changing very quickly, you need to take measurements very close together, otherwise you won't have enough data to make a decent graph.

Datalogging

Draw Different Kinds of Graphs

Most software will let you display your results in different ways.

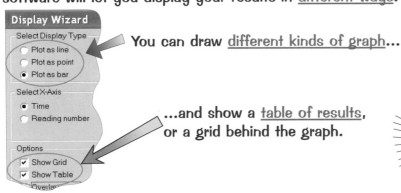

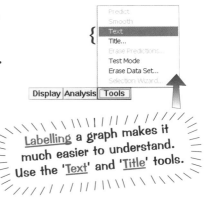

You can draw different kinds of graph...

...and show a table of results, or a grid behind the graph.

Labelling a graph makes it much easier to understand. Use the 'Text' and 'Title' tools.

Work Out What's Going On in the Graphs

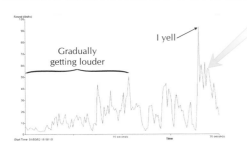

• This graph shows the noise level in my kitchen.

    • It gets gradually louder as people enter the room and start talking.

      • There's a big peak near the end where I dropped a hammer on my foot and yelled.

• This graph shows temperature levels in different places.

• It takes a while for the readings to 'settle down' in each new place — so the first reading isn't the most accurate.

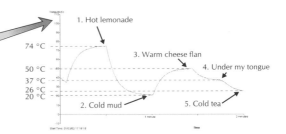

Save your Graphs, or Paste Them Somewhere

You might need to save your graphs — or paste them into a word processor.

Use the 'File' menu to save your graph.

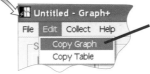

Use the 'Edit' menu to 'Copy' your graph.

Then you can paste it into a word processor like any other picture.

Which tennis player likes maths? — Steffi Graph...

The software does most things for you — it measures the temperature or sound levels, draws the graphs and so on. But you have to work out what's happening in the graphs. This means looking at the shape of the graph and interpreting it — i.e. thinking of reasons for its shape.

Instructions

Some things need a Single Instruction to Work

 Put your ticket in the machine...

The only instruction is "Raise the barrier".

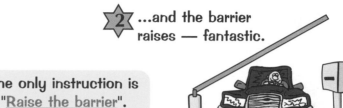 ...and the barrier raises — fantastic.

Some things need a Sequence of Instructions

This pelican crossing works using a sequence — one instruction changes the traffic lights and one changes the pedestrian lights.

Push the button...

...and the traffic lights go red and stop the cars...

...then the green walking man will appear — so walk.

Some things are Monitored and some are Timed

Computers can control different kinds of device and monitor the environment with sensors at the same time.

Timed events are where the computer turns things on and off at set times without monitoring the environment.

e.g. Computers monitor the surroundings, and turn a security light on if they detect movement or body heat.

e.g. Traffic lights stay red for 1 minute, then go green for 1 minute. It's a timed event.

You only need a single instruction: LEARN THIS PAGE

Learn the difference between timed events and events that happen due to a change in the environment. E.g. a traffic light that changes every two minutes without fail is timed, but one that changes when it detects a car approaching is monitoring the environment.

Inputs and Outputs

You can make your own programs to control things with a computer.
You'll need to use a <u>control box</u> though to connect all the bits together.

You Need a Control Box to Make Things Work

<u>Control boxes</u> connect the computer to <u>outputs</u> and <u>inputs</u>.

Inputs <u>get information</u>

Inputs: buttons, switches and levers, temperature, light and sound sensors...

Outputs <u>do things</u>

Outputs: lights, speakers, motors, buzzers, etc...

The inputs and outputs all have <u>numbers</u>.
This light bulb is plugged into "output 1".

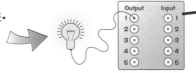

control box

Control Languages are in Charge of Control Boxes

When everything's attached, you can turn things <u>on</u> and <u>off</u> using a control language.

 Some control languages need to be <u>typed</u>.

```
Start
Turn output 1 on
Delay 5
Turn output 1 off
Stop
```

This switches on the light in output 1, then waits for a while, and switches it off again.

Other control programs work by getting you to draw a <u>flow chart</u>.

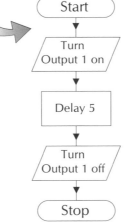

You have to put each line of your program in a certain <u>kind of box</u>.

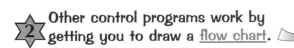
If the light was connected to <u>another output</u>, you'd use a different number, e.g. "turn output 3 on".

I'm fed up of taking orders — I'm off.

I know this stuff is exciting, but control yourself...

It doesn't matter what control software you have — they look a bit different but they all do the same thing. You might have to write something different, like "switch output 1 on", but your teacher will be able to explain all that to you.

Repeat and Wait

The <u>repeat</u> and <u>delay</u> commands make it quick and easy to create a <u>flashing light</u> output.

Flash your lights

If you want the light to flash, the "<u>Repeat</u>" command saves
you from having to turn it on and off over and over again.

Repeat makes things <u>happen again</u>.

You might write:

— repeats the thing in
brackets 10 times

Flow Charts
You <u>make loops</u>
to repeat things
in flow chart
programs.

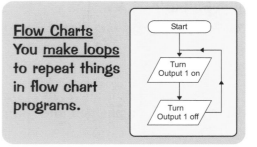

Use the DELAY (or WAIT) command

You can make the lights to stay on and off for longer by using the "<u>Delay</u>" (or "<u>Wait</u>") command.

So you might write:

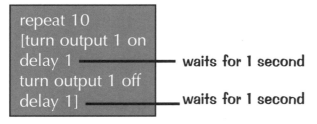

— waits for 1 second

— waits for 1 second

Flow Charts
Repeating a
section with some
delays in will look
a bit like this.

The procedure on this page is
called "<u>Flash</u>". It's a good idea to
name procedures, so you or
someone else knows what they do.

Right kids... This is the flow chart
for the next eight years of your lives.

Don't delay, use the flash procedure today...

A flashing light is a very useful output because it attracts attention more than a normal non-
flashing light would (that's why police cars have flashing lights). So it's good to learn how
to use the repeat and delay commands to create a flashing light output in the easiest way.

Repeat and Wait

Control languages use <u>procedures</u> that let you break your program into <u>smaller chunks</u>.

Repeat forever — makes an Endless Loop

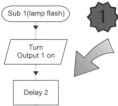

1 This <u>procedure</u> is called 'lamp flash'. It turns on the light in output 1 for 2 seconds, turns it off, then waits 2 seconds again before finishing.

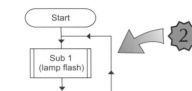

2 This <u>program</u> uses the procedure 'lamp flash' in an <u>endless loop</u>, i.e. the light flashes on and off forever.

3 The same program might look something like this in a typed control language:

```
repeat forever
lamp flash
end repeat
```

Check Inputs with a Decision Box or 'If... Then...'

Connecting a <u>switch</u> to your computer means the light will turn on <u>when the switch is pressed</u>.

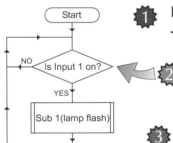

1 I've put my switch in input 1 — so check whether <u>input 1 is on</u>.

2 To check if input is on, use a <u>decision box</u>.

Decision boxes always have a 'yes' and a 'no' path leading from them.

3 If the switch is pressed, 'lamp flash' runs and the light flashes. If it isn't, the program loops round and checks again.

Or program might use an <u>if... then...</u> statement rather than a decision box.

```
repeat forever
if input 1 on then lamp flash
end repeat
```

Life is like an endless loop of decision boxes...

Once you've got some procedures written, you can make your program repeat them on an endless loop, so you don't need to do anything else to it ever again (unless you want to stop the loop, that is). Or you can use a switch to control whether a procedure happens or not.

Section Ten — Controlling Devices

Controlling Lots of Outputs

You can deal with different outputs <u>at the same time</u>. E.g. a program
could turn off a light and turn on a sound alarm at the same time.

You Can Control More Than One Output at a Time

You just type in...

> turn output 1 off
> turn output 2 on

...and it happens.

Storyboards Can Help You Plan Programs

It gets tricky when you have lots of outputs to think about. Writing a <u>storyboard</u>
helps you understand <u>which commands</u> you need to write into your program.

A traffic light storyboard might look like this:

BUT — you can be more precise, and write in <u>exactly</u> when each light goes on and off.

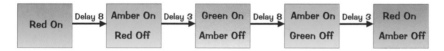

(This may not be how all traffic lights work, but this is about a
magic traffic light, and magic traffic lights are simpler than ours...)

The program could be written like this:

> turn output 1 on
> delay 8
> turn output 2 on
> turn output 1 off
> delay 3 etc...

Red   = Output 1
Amber = Output 2
Green = Output 3

The <u>flow chart</u> would
look like this...

Start

Turn Output 1 on

Delay 8

Turn Output 2 on

Turn Output 1 off

Let me tell you a storyboard...

Once upon a time, a girl was getting in a pickle with loads of outputs, so she wrote a
storyboard to help her see exactly what commands she had to write. The storyboard
helped her figure it out, and she lived happily ever after in a cottage by a stream. The end.

Controlling Lots of Outputs

Another way to avoid confusion is to write <u>procedures</u> for each <u>section</u> of your program.

Split your Programs into Sections

Splitting your program into sections makes it:

- easier to <u>understand</u>
- easier to <u>change bits</u>

E.g. a pelican crossing could have a <u>procedure</u> for each of these sections:

"NORMAL" → **"WALK"** → **"FLASH"**

Traffic is moving normally → Traffic stops and pedestrian walks → Lights flash before sequence ends and returns to "normal"

"NORMAL"
Traffic lights are green

Little man is red

"WALK"
The "wait" button is pressed by a pedestrian

The traffic lights go amber then red

The little man goes green

"FLASH"
The little green man flashes

The traffic lights flash amber

The little man turns red

The traffic lights turn green

Each <u>section</u> has its own <u>name</u>, to make them easier to keep track of.

> Your computer program might call procedures "<u>Sub-Programs</u>"
> or "<u>subs</u>". Don't worry — they're still the same thing...

You Can Repeat Each Section

You can repeat procedures as many times as you like by adding a "<u>repeat</u>" command.

You might write:

```
repeat 10
[sub 1]
```

"sub 1" means "run procedure 1".
This might change depending on <u>what program</u> you use.

In some programs, you enter the <u>name of your procedure</u>.
Your teacher will be able to tell you more...

```
repeat 10
[walk]
```

It's easier if you break it down into sec... ti... ons...

Splitting a big program up into different sections makes it easier — you can write a few simple procedures rather than one huge one. Also, if you need to change something, you can just think about the section that the change affects, not the whole thing.

Control Devices

Switches aren't the only kind of <u>input device</u>. There are some more <u>interesting ones</u> too.

Light Sensors can Tell when it gets Dark

<u>Light sensors</u> detect how much light there is.

- You can use a light sensor as a kind of <u>automatic switch</u> — instead of having to press a button to turn a light on, it comes on when it gets dark.

    - This is handy for lots of different things.

Light Sensors are Great for Making Lighthouses

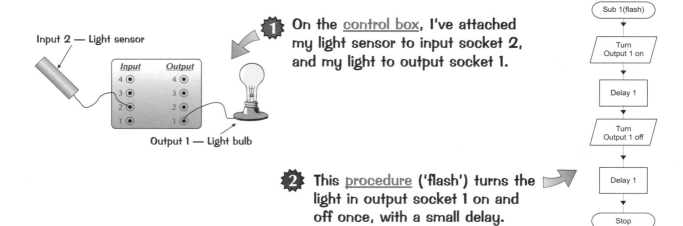

1 On the <u>control box</u>, I've attached my light sensor to input socket **2**, and my light to output socket **1**.

Input 2 — Light sensor

Output 1 — Light bulb

2 This <u>procedure</u> ('flash') turns the light in output socket 1 on and off once, with a small delay.

Sub 1(flash)
Turn Output 1 on
Delay 1
Turn Output 1 off
Delay 1
Stop

3 This <u>program</u> will make the light flash when it gets dark, but turn it off when it gets lighter.

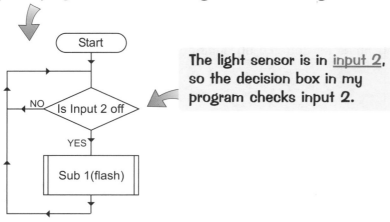

The light sensor is in <u>input 2</u>, so the decision box in my program checks input 2.

Let me enlighten you about light sensors...

A light sensor is similar to a switch, in that the program will only work when it's turned on. Switches have to be turned on by hand, but a light sensor will come on automatically.

Automatic Doors

You can attach more than one <u>input device</u> to a computer.

Pressure Pads <u>are a Different Kind of</u> Switch

• This automatic entrance door uses <u>pressure pads</u> to control when it opens and closes:

> A <u>heat sensor</u> or <u>light beam</u> could also be used to detect when somebody is coming.

When someone walks on the first pressure pad, the door opens...

...And when they walk on the second one, the door closes...

<u>Use</u> Procedures <u>to</u> Control <u>an Automatic Door</u>

The two procedures that control the door are called '<u>Open</u>' and '<u>Close</u>'.

'Open' turns <u>Motor A forward</u> to open the door — the motor runs for <u>half a second</u> and is then switched off:

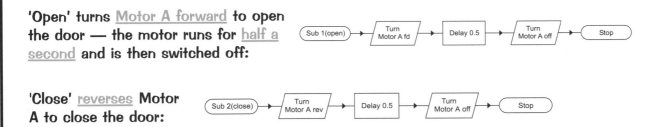

Sub 1(open) → Turn Motor A fd → Delay 0.5 → Turn Motor A off → Stop

'Close' <u>reverses</u> Motor A to close the door:

Sub 2(close) → Turn Motor A rev → Delay 0.5 → Turn Motor A off → Stop

<u>Then Use these Procedures in a</u> Program

This is the program that actually controls the door. Try to follow it <u>all</u>.

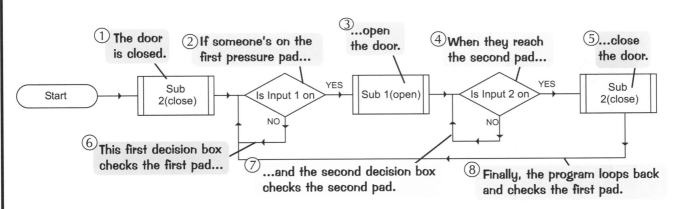

① The door is closed.
② If someone's on the first pressure pad...
③ ...open the door.
④ When they reach the second pad...
⑤ ...close the door.

Start → Sub 2(close) → Is Input 1 on — YES → Sub 1(open) → Is Input 2 on — YES → Sub 2(close)
NO / NO

⑥ This first decision box checks the first pad...
⑦ ...and the second decision box checks the second pad.
⑧ Finally, the program loops back and checks the first pad.

I can sense your pressure — chill out...

When you see the whole automatic doors program written down like this, it looks a bit scary. But don't panic — take a deep breath and break it down into all the different stages. Having two inputs doesn't make it harder, really. You just have a box for one, then a box for the other.

Problems Caused By Errors

You can write procedures to control as many inputs and outputs as you like, but it's <u>useless</u> if you leave important bits out or type something <u>daft</u>...

The Program _Only_ Does What _You Tell It_ To Do

A program will only work if you write it correctly. It's not like a human being.

> This is **GOOD** because it follows orders and doesn't get distracted.

> This is **BAD** because it can't make its own decisions and solve unexpected problems.

If you write a command to start doing something you <u>MUST</u> remember to tell it <u>when to stop</u>.

(...Or the school might explode...)

I'm sure there was something else I was meant to do...

So, be <u>really careful</u> not to leave any commands out.
Check they are all there and that the <u>lines that link them</u> are in the right place.

Be As _Organised_ As Possible. Always. Always. Always.

 1 The key things are <u>planning</u> and <u>double-checking</u> everything.

 2 <u>Test</u> what you've written before you use the procedure for real.

 3 It gets easier if you keep everything as <u>organised</u> as possible.

They told me to wait here. That was 3½ centuries ago...

THE <u>GOLDEN RULE</u> IS: NEVER START SOMETHING YOU CAN'T FINISH...

Never start something that you can't fi...

This page is basically just common sense. It's all fine and dandy learning about programs and learning to write fancy procedures, but there's no point even attempting these things until you've got these basic rules drummed into your head.

Index

A

address book 23
adventure games 56
alignment 2
alphabetical order 32, 36
analogue meter 63
'AND' searches 27, 44, 45
area formula 54
arrow keys 51
artwork 7
attachments 24
automatic doors 73
automatic switches 72
axes of graphs 39

B

BACK button 28
backspace 4
banks 47
bar charts 38
biased information 25, 47
Birmingham 45
blue eyes 37
bold 1
bookmark 29
branched keys 40
branching databases 40, 42
brush tool 10
budgets 50
buttons 17, 18, 28

C

capital letters 2
cartoons 7
CD-ROMs 16, 19, 28
cells 51, 52, 53, 54
centre aligned 2
charts and graphs
        39, 46, 49, 55, 65
chicken wallpaper 10
clear command 59
Clip-art 7, 12
commands 58, 59, 60
Compose World Junior 20
composing tunes 20
computer programming language
        59
continuous data 49
control boxes 67, 72
control devices 72

control languages 67, 69
copy 3, 10, 11, 30, 53
copyright 31
curry 37, 38
cut 3

D

databases 34, 36, 37,
        39, 42, 43, 47, 48
Data Harvest 63, 64
datalogging 64, 65
decision boxes 69, 73
delay (or wait) command 68
delete 4
digital camera 12
digital meter 63
drawing graphs 38, 39
drawing program 13, 14
drawing toolbar 13

E

easy maths 54
'Edit' menu 10, 11, 12
e-mail 22, 23, 24
e-mail addresses 22, 23
endless loops 69
equals sign 52
errors 48, 49, 74

F

favourites 29
fields 33, 37, 39, 43, 44
find and replace 5
finding patterns 57
'Find Next' 5
flashing light 68, 72
flight simulator 56
flip/rotate 11
floor turtle 58, 59
flow charts 67, 68, 70
formula bar 52
formulas 52, 53, 54
'Free Rotate' 14
font 1

G

'Graph' 63, 64
graph button 39
greater than 43

H

handles 7, 14
highlight 1, 3, 4, 55
hits 26
home command 59
homepage 17, 18
hotspots 17
hyperlinks 17, 28

I

'Image' menu 11
importing pictures 12
inbox 22
information 33, 35, 36, 38
input devices 72, 73
inputs and outputs 67, 70, 74
inserting pictures 7
instructions 9, 66
interactive 16
Internet 25, 26, 27, 28, 29, 30, 31,
        45, 47
interpreting graphs 65
italic 1

J

Junior Viewpoint 34, 37
justified text 2

K

keys 40

L

layers 14
left aligned text 2
less than 43
light sensors 72
lighthouses 72
line graphs 38, 49
linking pages 18
logo 9
LOGO 59, 61
loops 68

Index

M

machines 62
maths 54
melody 20
messy pile 32
Microsoft Excel 55
Microsoft Word 13
mistakes 47
modelling 15
mood of music 21
monitoring 62, 66
monsters 32
monsters' tea party 50
MS Paint 12
multimedia software 16
multiplication table 53
music notation 21
music software 20, 21
musical instruments 20
musical pictures 20, 21
musical sequence 20

N

new chart button 55
noise levels 62

O

object-based programs 13, 14
'OR' searches 44, 45
order 14
organising information 32
oriental music 21
outputs 67, 70, 71

P

packaging 9
painting software 10
paperclip 24
paste 3, 10, 11, 30, 53
paste from 12
patterns 10
pelican crossing 66
perimeter formula 54
photos 7, 9, 12
picture files 12
picture sets 20
pie charts 38, 39
planets and moons 43, 44
plot button 39
police databases 47

pressure pads 73
pretend 56
print 8, 22, 31
procedures
     61, 68, 69, 71, 72, 73, 74
punctuation marks 2
putting things in order 32

Q

questionnaires 35

R

real time 64
record cards 32, 33, 34
recording 19
records 33, 36, 48
remote data 64
repeat command 60, 68, 71
repeat forever command 69
research 25
rows and columns 51
right aligned text 2
rotate/flip 14

S

save 8
save as 8, 19
scanner 12
scatter graphs 46, 55
search button 37
search engines 26, 45
searches 26, 27, 43, 44, 45
searching a database 37, 43
sections 71
security lights 66
select tool 11
sending an e-mail 23
sensor unit 63
sensors 62, 63, 64
sequence of instructions 66
sequences 58
shapes of tree diagrams 41
shift key 2
silly data 48
simulations 56
single instruction 66
skimming 27
snapshot mode 64
songs 20
sort button 36

sorting information 36
sound file 19
sound levels 62
Sound Recorder 19
special symbols 2
spell-checkers 6
spreadsheet table 55
spreadsheets 51, 54, 55
stamper tool 10
storing sound 19
storyboards 70
sub-programs 71
SUM 53
surfing the Internet 28

T

tempo 20
testing new inventions 56
theme of music 21
thermostats 62
tick boxes 35
timed events 66
traffic lights 66, 70
training pilots 56
train timetable 48
tree diagrams 40, 41, 42
tunes menu 20
typed commands 67
turtle 58, 59
typing mistakes 48

U

underline 1
undo 11
URLs 29, 30

V

velociraptor 27
virtual pets 56
volume control 19

W

weather forecasters 62
website address 29
websites 25, 26, 28, 29, 45
web pages 16
Windows Explorer 19
Windows Sound Recorder 19